∽ ∾

Reclaim Your Spiritual Power

∽ ∾

Also by Ron Roth, Ph.D.

Books

(with Peter Occhiogrosso)
The Healing Path of Prayer
Holy Spirit*
Holy Spirit for Healing*
I Want to See Jesus in a New Light*
Prayer and the Five Stages of Healing*
(also available in Spanish)

Audios

The Dark Night of the Soul*
The Healing Path of Prayer
Healing Prayers*
Holy Spirit: The Boundless Energy of God*
Prayer and Spirit As Energy Medicine*
Prayer and the Five Stages of Healing*

All of the above are available
at your local bookstore.
Items with asterisks may also be ordered
through Hay House, Inc.:

(800) 654-5126 or **(760) 431-7695**
(800) 650-5115 (fax) or **(760) 431-6948 (fax)**
www.hayhouse.com

Reclaim Your Spiritual Power

Ron Roth, Ph.D.,
with Peter Occhiogrosso

Hay House, Inc.
Carlsbad, California • Sydney, Australia
Canada • Hong Kong • United Kingdom

Published and distributed in the United States by:
Hay House, Inc., P.O. Box 5100, Carlsbad, CA 92018-5100
(800) 654-5126 • (800) 650-5115 (fax) • www.hayhouse.com
Hay House Australia Pty Ltd, P.O. Box 515, Brighton-Le-
Sands, NSW 2216 • *phone:* 1800 023 516 • *e-mail:* info@hayhouse.com.au

Editorial supervision: Jill Kramer • *Design:* Julie Davison

Library of Congress Cataloging-in-Publication Data

Roth, Ron.
      Reclaim your spiritual power / Ron Roth with Peter Occhiogrosso.
            p. cm.
      ISBN 1-56170-708-2
      1. Spiritual life. I. Occhiogrosso, Peter. II. Title.
      BL624 .R68 2002
      291.4'4—dc21

                                                    2002000810

                              ISBN 1-56170-708-2

              05 04 03 02   4 3 2 1
              1st printing, August 2002

          Printed in the United States of America

*For all those individuals whose prayers
and expressions of love hastened my swift
return to health, and my renewed dedication
to experience life more fully in the spirit of
St. Irenaeus, who stated, "The glory of God
is found in the person who is fully alive."*

*My sincere, heartfelt thanks to all of you,
including the staffs of Hoag Hospital
in Newport Beach, California; and Illinois
Valley Community Hospital in Peru, Illinois,
and to my personal physician, Dr. Kim.*

*God bless you all. I will never forget
your kindness to me.*

Contents

꒰ꐕ꒱

Introduction

∽ ও ৎৎ

Changing Our Misconceptions

"The search for yourself is your life's purpose. To know yourself is to know the power of God within you. We are here to discover our truth and to make our unique contribution to life. The Spirit wants us to give something back to health and to heal others, but first the healing must begin within us. We must learn to trust the mystic within. We must learn to recognize and respect God within ourselves. You and I know these truths. We know the way. Our challenge is to close the book, to leave the religious service, to turn off the tape, and practice living the message. The more we practice living from within, listening and talking to God throughout each day, the more conscious we become of God's indwelling presence. The more receptive our minds and hearts become to the wisdom of Spirit, then we have deeper insights and a greater understanding of life. Then our duties, cares, and worries become our opportunities for growth and our burdens become lighter."

— Susan Taylor, *In the Spirit*

*I*n the 1970s and '80s, I often experienced periods of intense depression . . . even though I was a Catholic priest. To try to help change my frame of mind, I would go to hear motivational speakers, and each time I did, I felt so good immediately afterwards—but then I would find myself returning to my depressed state just a few days later. I still believe that this happens to most of us when we go to hear inspirational lecturers or motivational speakers, because we fail to realize that authentic motivation does not come from somebody else. Our most powerful and authentic inspiration originates *from within us.*

As I preached to hundreds of people every Sunday, I began to notice that I would go from one extreme to the other. Sometimes I was very "gung ho" about my religious duties and prayer life, often praying three to four hours every day—this was very invigorating for me, but if I didn't also take care of my body with exercise and nutrition, I couldn't maintain that level of energy. But then, after hearing someone like the motivational speaker John Bradshaw, I would remind myself that something in my inner make-up needed to be dealt with. So I would work on some psychological aspect of myself, letting go of the prayer, exercise, and diet; and once again, I would become bored.

This vicious circle continued until one day it finally hit me: To be congruent and in harmony, and to live a healthy, holistic life, you have to work on all three areas of yourself at the same time—your spiritual essence, your emotional and psychological being, and your body.

One story from the Gospels eventually changed my understanding of how we limit our view of what we need to be whole. The Master Jesus comes to a town and notices a blind man sitting there. Jesus asks the man what he would like Jesus to do for him. The man replies, "That I might see." Jesus says "See!" That was it—he walked away and the man saw.

In another section of the Gospel, however, the Master enters a different city and comes across yet another blind man. Jesus asks him what the problem is, and the man says, "I cannot see and I want to." This time, Jesus spits on the ground, makes a mud ball, and plasters it on the man's eyes. He asks the man if he can see now. But the man is honest and says, "Well, no, not really. People look like trees moving around." Then, like any good spiritual master would, Jesus ministers to him again, and this time the man is finally able to see clearly.

Nowhere in the Gospel does Jesus pray for the sick the way you and I were taught to pray. He doesn't ask God to heal anyone. Instead, he customizes the healing to each situation and simply commands the healing to take place. One day I began to wonder if the two blind men in those accounts ever met. I imagined that, about a year and a half later, Jesus is coming to town to give a lecture, and both of these formerly blind men happen to show up. They don't know each other, because they weren't in the same town when they were healed. But people are gathering because the Master is about to teach and heal the sick— and the word gets around that these two have already been healed by Jesus. So the two men meet.

The first man says to the other, "I hear that he healed you."

"That's right," the other one replies.

"Oh, I know what's that like. I can remember the day he came along and said, 'See!'"

And the second man says, "No, no, that's not the way he did it at all! He spit on my eyes and he healed me, but it took him two tries."

The first one says, "Nonsense! He just asked me what my trouble was, but he didn't use any spit or mud."

But the second man holds to his conviction that it takes spit and mud to heal blindness. And that's how the first denominations began: the Mudites and the Anti-Mudites.

Today, we do much the same thing as I imagined those two blind men doing. We've been programmed to believe that things can happen only one way, within one context. Healing, we believe, requires a very holy person, with *holiness*

defined a particular way: To some people, it means being pious, folding your hands, and mumbling a canned prayer. But the roots of the English word *holy* are the same as for *whole* and *health*. So to be authentically holy, you need to be a complete person. You can't live in the etheric realm and pretend you don't have a body. I like the definition given by the fourth-century mystic St. Irenaeus: "The glory of God is found in the person who is fully alive." That means being filled with joy, enthusiasm, zest for living, love, and passion.

Being "whole" means using all the resources available to you—outer and inner, material and spiritual, logical and intuitive, allopathic and holistic. This represents the balance that can make you whole, and therefore, healthy and holy as well. Anything less is a misconception.

Yet sometimes we have to be awakened to the fact that the spiritual power we need to heal is already available to us. The Gospel of John (5:1-9) tells the story of a man who had been an invalid for many years. For much of that time, this man had been coming to the well at Bethesda in a vain attempt to heal himself. The local superstition held that the moment the water began to ripple in this pond, it signaled that the angel of God had brushed it, and then the first one into the pool would be healed.

When Jesus saw the man lying there and learned that he had had this condition for a long time, the Master asked him, "Do you want to be whole?"

"Sir," the invalid replied, "I have no one to help me into the pool when the water is stirred. Whenever I try to get in, someone else goes down ahead of me."

You get the feeling that this man had long since given up expecting to be healed. He had stopped taking responsibility for his life, so he was just going through the motions. If he had nobody to carry him to the pool, then he felt that he had no chance of being healed, even by superstition. How do I know this? Because when Jesus came up to him, the man began to make excuses. He made himself out to be a victim, yet he didn't explain why, if he had nobody to put him in the pool, he hadn't realized the futility of his situation and moved on.

So Jesus said to him, "Get up! Pick up your mat and walk." And the Gospel tells us that the man was cured at once.

This individual had been doing what most of us do at some point or another—playing the role of the victim. But Jesus wouldn't let him do that anymore. He put the guy on the spot by asking if he wanted to heal or not. In psychological terms, Jesus interrupted this man's thought patterns. Although Zen did not develop until long after Jesus was gone, here he acted like a Zen master who startles someone outside of their everyday mental routine and "surprises" them into healing.

Paul Reps gives an example of this in his classic book, *Zen Flesh, Zen Bones: A Collection of Zen and Pre-Zen Writings.* Reps tells the story of the Japanese master Nan-in and a younger monk named Tenno, who had recently passed his apprenticeship to become a teacher of Zen himself.

One rainy day, Tenno visited Nan-in and parked his umbrella alongside his wooden clogs before going in to see the master.

After greeting him, Nan-in remarked, "I suppose you left your wooden clogs in the vestibule. I want to know if your umbrella is on the right or left side of the clogs."

Tenno, confused, had no instant answer. He realized that he was unable to carry his Zen every minute of every day. Nan-in jolted the younger man into realizing that he was not fully conscious at each moment of his life. Tenno realized that he was not ready to become a teacher—so he became Nan-in's pupil, and studied six more years to accomplish his "every-minute Zen."

The apostle Peter did much the same thing as Nan-in when, on his way into a prayer meeting, he encountered a paralyzed man begging for alms. Peter told the man that he didn't have silver or gold, but he did have the power to heal. He then loudly commanded the man to stand up . . . and the man was healed. The paralytic didn't have time to think about it, and the channel to healing was opened up—just as the channel to insight or enlightenment can be opened by a Zen master's unexpected comment or action.

For me, personally, awakening to that same level of awareness and reclaiming my own innate spiritual power required two events that, although seemingly unrelated, bear a direct spiritual relationship to each other. Moreover, these two extraordinary events fell very closely in time on either side of one of the most cataclysmic events of our time—the terrorist attacks of September 11, 2001. I hope that by telling you the story of these happenings, I can begin to show you how to reclaim the vast spiritual power that already lies within you.

Chapter One

∽ ✑ ∾

How I Reclaimed My Own Spiritual Power

*I*n August of 2001, I traveled to Brazil with four companions to visit a miraculous healer named Joao de Deus, or "John of God." Joao's healing work is the kind that gives skeptics headaches: For the past 30 years, he has treated more than 1,000 people a day, close to 11 million in all. He performs both visible and invisible operations (I'll explain more about these later in the chapter), reportedly healing paraplegics, the blind, and more than 100 cases of AIDS. A medium as well as a healer, Joao accomplishes all of this while in trance, during which he incorporates one or more spirit entities who were themselves remarkable healers, physicians, surgeons, psychologists, or theologians during their lives, but who now operate exclusively on the spirit plane. John of God has made contact with more than 30 of these spirit beings, including: Ignatius Loyola, who founded the Jesuit order in the 16th century and later traveled to Brazil; Oswaldo Cruz, who eradicated yellow fever in Brazil in the early 20th century; and Dr. Augusto de Almeida, a Brazilian physician and surgeon about whom little is known. These entities help Joao in his healing work in much the same way that I've experienced the presences of Padre Pio, St. Martin de Porres, and Sister Faustina during my own healing services (which I describe in my book *Prayer and the Five Stages of Healing*).

Joao de Deus has been persecuted by the medical establishment and police force of Brazil due to his unconventional methods. I find this to be incredible, for although it isn't widely known outside of church circles, Roman Catholic theology includes the concept of a "communion of saints," which is one of its most mystical ideas. As defined in the new *Catechism of the Catholic Church* (item 962, taken from an encyclical by Pope Paul VI), Catholics "believe in the communion of all the faithful of Christ, those who are pilgrims on earth, the dead who are being purified, and the blessed in heaven, all together forming one Church; and we believe that in this communion, the merciful love of God and his saints is always [attentive] to our prayers." As I understand the truth behind this statement to say, the spirits of highly realized beings who have passed over to the other world are available to help those of us still in physical form, although we may often be unaware or only dimly aware of their presence. For example, Padre Pio (the 20th-century Catholic priest and mystic) and Thérèse of Lisieux (known as the "Little Flower") both said that they would be able to do much more for humanity from the other side than they could in the physical realm. Thérèse, who died at the age of 24, told those around her, "I want to spend my heaven doing good on earth." When Padre Pio was dying, the people where he lived feared that all the good work he had begun would come to an end, the pilgrims would dwindle, and the local hospital would experience financial trouble. Instead, as Father Stefano Manelli writes in *Padre Pio of Pietrocina*, "The opposite happened. Padre Pio had said some years before, 'I will make more noise when I am dead than when I was alive.' Also 'In Paradise I will work with both hands.'" And St. Dominic, who founded the Order of Preachers in the early 13th century, told his religious brothers on his deathbed, "Do not weep, for I shall be more useful to you after my death and I shall help you more effectively than during my life."[1]

Despite his oppression, John of God continues his healing work in a house in central Brazil. He had learned of my own healing work through one of my clients, and he was kind enough to invite me to visit him and observe his work during his healing services. As it happens, I had become familiar with Joao's work from a book called *The Miracle Man: The Life Story of Joao de Deus* by Robert Pellegrino-Estrich,[2] which I had read about a year before my trip to Brazil. I had also seen a video of Joao's work that touched my spirit deeply, so I was certainly eager to meet the man.

I was not disappointed. During the ten days I spent with Joao, I had the profound feeling that I had come home spiritually. I had left the Catholic priesthood 10 years before, after 25 years of service, and even though this had freed me in many ways, I had often felt like a fish out of water. It has been quite frustrating for me at times because I haven't known exactly what my calling is. But while I was in Brazil, I began to get back in touch with the essence of my personal journey. I spent at least five hours a day in prayer, and many hours working with Joao. I became alive again watching him work wonders, all the while giving credit to God for the work. Even though Joao employs a somewhat different form of healing than I do, when I was in his presence, it became clear to me that we've long been brothers in the world of Spirit.

Joao and I often prayed together, and as I watched him use his spiritual gifts, I knew that I had the same gifts but had stopped fully using them in large gatherings or retreats for the past ten years. Sure, I had allowed healing to manifest, but I had left prophecy behind. I had also stopped using what are known as "words of knowledge and wisdom," which are prescriptions for cures that people could apply after leaving me. In addition, I had given up performing "invisible operations." This is a technique where no skin is cut or blood is shed, but people begin to feel certain parts of their bodies being "operated" on—as strange as this may sound to some, it's the way the Holy Spirit operates. Joao also had that gift. It was absolutely inspiring to be around him.

One Sunday, Joao invited me to say a healing mass for anyone who wanted to attend. I no longer follow the rites of the Roman Catholic Church; instead, I just allow the Spirit to operate through me while I perform sacramental rituals. So we broke loaves of bread, drank wine, said healing prayers, and sang and chanted for more than three hours. As Joao had invited me to observe and give validation to his healing work, he, in turn, took a seat in the congregation to do the same for me.

I became certain that I was about to return to the path I had once followed, because it was my purpose in life to use these graces and gifts to manifest the presence and glory of God. Rather than talk about healing, as I had been doing, I needed to model what I believe—which is the God Spirit operating in this world and through each of us. This means that I'm an extension of the Divine Spirit—I'm a son of God, an individual who's an heir to the energy of Jesus Christ, as all of us are. After all, Jesus came to Earth to demonstrate what we all could become, that we could all do what he did, and I was *not* fulfilling this mission.

And so, after returning to the United States, I began to rethink the weeklong intensive work-shop that I was scheduled to give in San Diego in mid-September. I now knew that I wanted to do more prayer work with the participants, and I was ready to employ whatever graces God permitted me to use; perhaps I could even write out Divine prescriptions for individual healings or whisper to people some of the things that were keeping them from being healed. Padre Pio had the gift of reading hearts—that is, he could look at people and know from the Divine Spirit within them what was blocking their healing, which often included incidents from their past that they had to let go of so that they could get on with their lives. This was a gift I had been blessed with as well, and I wanted to use it again.

Although I wasn't fully aware of it at the time, those days I spent with Joao in Brazil represented the first step in reclaiming the spiritual power that I had begun to lose.

A Stroke of Luck

I was scheduled to fly to San Diego on September 13. On the morning of September 11, I called my collaborator, Peter, to begin wrapping

up what was to be the text of this book. He was
the first to inform me of the horrific events that
had just begun to unfold at the World Trade
Center and the Pentagon, and questioned
whether I would be able to fly to San Diego at all,
since commercial flights had been grounded
indefinitely following the terrorist hijackings.
Since we didn't know how things would turn
out, we agreed to postpone work on the book.
And sure enough, my flight had been canceled,
as were several subsequent bookings I tried to
make. In the end, I was forced to charter a small
jet to fly me from my hometown of Peru, Illinois,
to San Diego. Anxiety over my uncertain travel
plans, combined with my grief and sadness over
the terrorist attacks and the great loss of life, left
me feeling disoriented and vulnerable.

And yet, during the five-day prayer retreat,
it was evident that my renewed commitment to
God was beginning to bear fruit. I found myself
teaching without hearing or even knowing what
I was saying, as I felt the Spirit of God speak
through me. I began by talking about what the

nation had just experienced, and we all prayed for our country. I spontaneously returned to writing out Divine prescriptions for people, often in the form of scriptural passages, to help bring each individual more swiftly into a realm of healing. I went down into the audience to give prophetic words to people, sharing with them what I saw, on a clairvoyant level, as certain steps they needed to take in order to heal. Once again, I began to pray in tongues. When this happens, I bypass my own mind and connect with the Spirit of God, and I usually speak or sing in a heavenly language that's unintelligible to others. I hadn't done this publicly for many years.

I also allowed myself to return to deliverance work, casting out various negative energies that I spoke of in *Prayer and the Five Stages of Healing*. I had stopped talking about these dangerous elementals (as they're known in mystical literature), perhaps feeling that it was "spiritually incorrect" to focus on the negative in any way. Yet I now realized that these energies do overtake people, and they need to be dealt with openly and fearlessly. All in all, the retreat was an enormous breakthrough for me, on both a spiritual and personal level.

After the intensive was over, some of us stayed on at the hotel for a few days. While I was teaching at the Church of Religious Science in North Hollywood, my associate Paul Funfsinn noticed that I had begun to slur some of my words. This had totally escaped me, although I was aware after going swimming the next day that I was getting very tired for no apparent reason. I fell asleep on the chaise longue, and when I woke up, I felt weak and was still tired. As the day progressed, I began to feel as if I was slipping out of my body altogether. The thought occurred to me that this is what it must feel like to go into a coma. By the next morning, I was slipping deeper into that feeling of coma . . . and then I felt my left arm go completely dead. It just hung at my side. Not long after that, my left leg gave out and my foot began to drag behind me—it was so bad that Paul and another colleague, Bruce Baumgatner, had to hold me up.

I called a holistic doctor who is a good friend, and when I described my symptoms, he commanded me to get to the nearest hospital emergency room immediately. "Why?" I said. "It's probably just the flu."

"No," he said. "I think you're having a stroke."

I was totally stunned and began to cry. "Why is this happening to me?" I inquired of nobody in particular. But before I could come up with an answer, Paul and Bruce had loaded me into a car and we were on our way to the emergency room of Hoag Hospital in Newport Beach. I decided to stop complaining to the heavens; and right then and there, I put my faith in God and the doctors and nurses at Hoag, and surrendered to whatever was to happen.

The news was actually pretty good. After four days in the hospital—much to the surprise and delight of the medical staff—my left arm and leg had begun to come back gradually, and I was released into the care of Becky and Chris Prelitz, a couple of friends in the area. Becky is a dietitian and nutritionist who immediately began teaching me how to eat more healthful, balanced meals.

Prior to leaving for Brazil, I had restarted my exercise program and had at least begun to get my body in shape, but my diet was as poor as ever. The stroke was a potent wake-up call telling me emphatically that it wasn't enough for me to be preaching about holistic living: I was going to have to start *living* that way myself.

I was also fortunate to have thousands of people praying for me after word of my stroke got out to the prayer circles I've been involved with. For some time, I had been helping Paul and Bruce learn how to be channels for the healing energy of the Holy Spirit by simply being still. Now they were able to channel the love and peace and concern of all those people praying for me so that it reached my body. They were like magnifying lenses focusing and intensifying sunlight by putting their hands on me while repeating the intention, "Come, Holy Spirit." Life energy flowed through them and focused on the parts of my body where I most needed healing.

But I also had to do my part. I had allowed my schedule to become much too busy, not because I needed the money, but because I liked all the attention and the exchange of energy that I get from a group—and because the kind of work I do generates a momentum of its own, which can be hard to step back from. I knew that my healing wouldn't come quickly unless I canceled my schedule for a couple of months. Instead of charging around the country from workshop to retreat, I would have to relax, meditate, and surrender to God's perfect plan for my life.

During that time of recuperation and relaxation, my prayer life once again began to take greater precedence in my life, and at the same time, I felt a stronger connection than ever before with the other side. I was able to go in and out of meditative trances more frequently and peacefully, and I even sensed the presence of a new entity with whom I had never before worked, encouraging me to heal myself. The occupational and physical therapists and my medical doctors kept telling me that my recuperation was going remarkably fast. I soon recovered the use of my left arm and leg to a large extent, and my speech returned to normal.

While I was focusing on recovery, I sent an e-mail to an assistant of Joao de Deus in Brazil, asking if Joao could learn from the entities he worked with what the reason was for my stroke. My question was presented to Joao while he was in trance during his healing work. The entity known as Dr. Augusto Almeida replied through Joao that the reason for the stroke was that I was passing over to the other side. I had been dying and didn't know it! My feeling of going into a state of coma at that time, the sensation of my spirit leaving my body, represented what was actually happening and *would* have happened. Through Joao, Dr. Augusto said, "Father Ron was going to the other world. I said that I would work with Father Ron so that he could complete his mission on Earth." I took his statement to mean that he had somehow intervened to keep me in this world for a time.

It suddenly struck me that my remarkable recovery in the hospital, and my renewed awareness of the entities I have depended on from the other side, had a much deeper purpose than I had imagined. Those entities were there to help me directly. I had felt their presence in the hospital, although I couldn't attach a name to the new entity I became aware of after I got home. But I have since seen a picture of Dr. Augusto, and I realized that it was indeed he.

❧

After September 11, so many people have lamented, with a mixture of sadness and dread, that our lives will never be the same again. That's true for me as well, although the events of that tragic day are only a small part of the reason. I truly can never be the same, nor can my work. All that I can do, from this point on, is to model the presence of God and do what I can for suffering humanity, especially at this trying time in the history of our nation and the world. Since my stroke, I've been invited to India and Austria and other places abroad, and I know this to be a signal from God to model the presence and power of Him wherever I am.

I'm also more aware than ever before that I'm an imperfect creature, but I do what I can, in consideration of my own limitations, to fulfill my mission with as much love as possible. I try to help the brothers and sisters who suffer and seek me out. I never claim to cure anyone, because I know that it's *God* who cures, in whatever form He sees best in His infinite kindness. I'm only a tool in God's hands. If He chooses one form over another, that's God's business, not mine. As Jesus says in the Gospel of John (15:12): "This is my commandment which I give to you: love one another as I have loved you."

My experience with John of God and my stroke and recovery have added immeasurably to the spiritual insights that I had already begun to communicate in this book. I've since gone back and revisited everything that I had previously written, passing it through the filter of my new awareness. But the title and theme of this book remain the same. Indeed, it now seems to me in retrospect to be about the process of spiritual reclamation that I began to undergo myself only after I had begun to write it! It's almost as though some spiritual editor had insisted that I go back and rethink my approach and revise my manuscript based on a much more personal experience of regaining spiritual power. And for that, I can only be grateful.

[1] *Catechism of the Catholic Church,* New York: Image, 1995, pp. 271–273.

[2] Robert Pellegrino-Estrich, *The Miracle Man: The Life Story of Joao de Deus,* Cairns, Queensland, Australia: Triad, 2001.

Chapter Two

∽ ∾

The Seven Components
of Empowerment

*T*here's nothing magical about the process of reclaiming your spiritual power, even though empowerment can seem elusive at times. Through many years of personal experience and working with others for healing, I've determined that certain traits and areas of emphasis are essential to liberating the spiritual energy that lies dormant in most of us. To take some of the mystery out of this process, I've boiled the most valuable components of empowerment down to just seven. These traits, virtues, or attitudes (or however you choose to characterize them) help us to heal and keep us healthy, even though they don't appear to be directly related to health and fitness. The easiest way to help you get started is to go through them one at a time. They are:

1. Positive Beliefs
2. Vision (Purpose in Life)
3. Imagination and Creativity
4. Passion
5. Language
6. Gratitude
7. Forgiveness

1. Positive Beliefs

For a long time now, I've followed this simple series of premises that shows how positive beliefs lead to beneficial results:

- Programming creates beliefs.
- Beliefs create attitudes.

- Attitudes create feelings.
- Feelings determine action.
- Action creates results.

Your beliefs not only empower you, they can also disempower you. You may, for example, have been programmed to believe that life is meant to be a struggle. Your parents or your life situation may have taught you to never plan on anything because it won't work out— and, so, that's exactly what will manifest in your life. If that's the case, then perhaps you'll need to examine what you actually believe about God, other people, life in general, and health in particular.

What you believe comes from your thoughts, which stems from your programming. This is why the mystics of different religions all advise us to watch what we think. "As one thinks in his heart, so is he," says the Book of Proverbs (23:7), which dates from around 1,000 B.C. Some 500 years later, the Buddha said much the same thing:

All states have mind as their forerunner, mind is their chief, and they are mind-made. If one speaks or acts with a defiled mind, then suffering follows one even as the wheel follows the hoof of the draft-ox. . . . If one speaks or acts with a pure mind, happiness follows as one's shadow that does not leave one.

(*Dhammapada,* 1–2)

When you apply this construct to healing, it can have unintended results. If you come to a healing service or workshop, for instance, you may believe, *I'm here to learn how to heal other people, because God wants to heal others.* That sounds reasonable enough, but if *you're* the one who needs healing, it's not going to do you much good. Yet people often tell me that they've come to one of my healing services so that I can help whomever they've brought with them. "I'm here for *her*," a woman will say, pointing to her friend. "So please help her. Pray for her."

If I ask this woman about her own needs, she'll invariably insist that she doesn't need prayer herself because her friend, parent, child, or spouse is sicker than she is. That kind of thinking implies that God has only enough energy for one healing at a time—such as those promotional offers that are only "one to a household."

As the old saying goes, "Give a man a fish and you feed him for a day. *Teach* a man to fish and you feed him for life." I'm less interested in healing your body, emotions, or spirit than I am in teaching you principles that will allow you to heal your life—your *entire* life. Because if you don't set out to heal your life in its totality, you probably won't succeed in healing any part of it at all. What good is it to heal your body but still be unhappy? That's like repainting your house but forgetting to fix the crumbling foundation. Beliefs are the foundation, the building blocks, for creating your life. Positive beliefs will help you transcend any difficulty.

In the Christian Testament, Jesus says, "With God all things are possible." But he also says, "If you believe, nothing shall be impossible for *you*" (my italics). I may feel empowered when I think that God can do something for me, but if my beliefs say He will do it for someone else but not for me, I won't be empowered for long. I have to believe and have confidence that nothing is impossible for *me*.

2. Vision (*Purpose in Life*)

There were times during the onset of my stroke (and just afterward, too) that my beliefs weren't terribly positive. I began to think that this was the end of my physical health. So when I recovered, I realized that I must be here for a purpose that's larger than what I had previously assumed. Prior to my visit to Joao de Deus in Brazil, I thought that I was "on purpose," but now I see that I wasn't. As much as I enjoy teaching, for instance, I no longer consider that to be my purpose in life. My real purpose is to lead people to God, which may happen through teaching or healing—but those are merely vehicles for that higher purpose.

My relationship with God—and the modeling of that relationship through the use of my spiritual graces in public—helps to bring healing to individuals and to the planet as a whole. When I spent time with Joao, I watched him go into trance as people lined up in front of him for healing. Among other things, he would often write out the names of the herbs that each individual needed for healing. As I watched him do this, I recalled that I used to work in much the same mode years ago, giving out what I call "Divine prescriptions." Sometimes I would intuitively write a scriptural passage for the person who needed healing, giving just the chapter and verse. The idea was for the person to look up the passage, which would offer insight into the health challenge he or she was facing. When I left the priesthood, I abandoned that practice, perhaps believing that it was somehow too closely connected to church rituals or that it was presumptuous of me if I was no longer in the priesthood. Now, however, I realize that denying my graces or intuitive gifts wasn't an act of humility—they're part of my purpose for being here, and to experience fulfillment, I would have to use them all.

The Book of Proverbs (29:18) says, "Without a vision, the people perish." Without a mission or a purpose, you'll go nowhere. You'll end up scattering your energies, feeling depleted, and having no power or authority. One time when I was still a parish priest, I wanted to prove the impact that words and beliefs can have. During a Sunday sermon, I said, "We're going to take a test today. I want everyone to get relaxed and I'll just list a few words. When I'm done, I'm going to share with you what this test was about." So I said these words: *dumb, stupid, joyless, grouchy, crummy, low-down, worm, dust.* As I watched my audience that Sunday, I could see the energy drain out of them. With some people it was subtle, but with others, I could see them slump in their seats with their heads sinking into their chests.

Then I started another list of words: *joy, peace, strength, power, confidence, love.* I could see a few heads rise up and could feel their spirits lifting as well. By the time I was done, smiles had lit up some of those same faces that had been sagging just a moment before.

Try the same exercise on yourself: Look in the mirror and speak first the negative and then the positive sets of words listed above to your image, and see what effect that has on your body. Pay attention to how the words make you *feel*. Watch your own mind as if you're watching a movie—because thoughts and images will flit through your mind as quickly as words and pictures on a movie screen. You'll probably hear yourself adding a commentary to the words: *Yeah, I'm dumb all right. Why did I agree to do this ridiculous exercise? I don't need this to make me feel like a jerk!*

After you've finished, remain aware of how often you use negative or positive words throughout the day to describe yourself or others. "Jeez! What a clumsy thing to do!" Or, "Ooh, that was so stupid!" Will any of that mental chatter really help you overcome your lack of coordination or perception? We all do this to ourselves, but we have to stop—because if we continue, our clumsiness and thoughtlessness actually will increase. We have to let go of our constant self-judging and envision how good our lives can be, because without that vision, negativity will rush in to fill the gap, and we will indeed perish.

3. Imagination and Creativity

Perhaps a story will help you see more clearly how I used these principles myself when I first started working with the sick. I tried very hard to teach people how to bring these concepts into their own lives so they could help heal themselves.

There's a tale in the Hebrew Bible that carries one of the most powerful motivational messages I've ever read. It isn't about sin or piety or religious observance, but about the power of the *imagination*, and I read this story a dozen times over a couple of years before I finally got it. It's the story of Jacob and Laban, which stretches over several chapters in the Book of Genesis (29–31).

Jacob had been laboring for Laban, his uncle, tending his flocks of sheep and goats for seven years to win the hand of Laban's younger daughter, Rachel. But when the seven years were up, Laban tricked Jacob into taking his older daughter, Leah, instead. Jacob objected after the fact, so Laban offered to let him marry Rachel as well . . . if he worked for him for another seven years. Jacob did so, and one day, he got an inspiration. Jacob approached Laban with a plan that sounded as if it would make Laban even richer at Jacob's expense.

Jacob told Laban, "Let me go through all of your flocks today and remove from them every speckled or spotted sheep, every dark-colored lamb, and every spotted or speckled goat. They will be my wages."

Laban agreed, perhaps because the dark or spotted animals were valued less than the solid-colored ones or because there were fewer of them. Anyway, Laban went out and formed a flock for Jacob, which consisted of all the sheep and goats that were ringed, spotted, or had white patches. All of the black sheep he gave to Jacob's sons to take on the three-day hike into the distance to Jacob. Jacob then stayed and cared for Laban's flock. At one point, he took fresh shoots growing out of the ground from poplar, almond, and plane trees and peeled white streaks into them. He put spotted and speckled indentations in the branches and placed them beside the watering troughs so that the flocks would see them when they went to drink, for that's when they copulated.

When the flocks mated before the streaked rods, their offspring were streaked and spotted, and Jacob added them to his flock. Then Jacob divided out the ewes from Laban's flock and segregated them from the rams and let them mate only with Jacob's black rams, so he built his own flocks of sheep from Laban's. Moreover, Jacob waited until the stronger animals were ready to mate, and then he placed the peeled branches before them so the stronger animals would produce speckled offspring and the weaker livestock would produce solid-colored offspring. The weak and sickly lambs belonged to Laban, and the stronger ones were Jacob's. As a result, Jacob's flocks increased rapidly and he became very wealthy, with many servants, camels, and donkeys.

This story is about the power of the imagination to create. I initially thought that it was the cows and the sheep that were visualizing the colors, thereby producing spotted and speckled offspring. What I didn't understand is that *Jacob* was using something tangible to envision spotted and speckled animals—it was his visualization that increased his flocks.

In the following chapter, Laban's sons have become indignant over Jacob's good fortune, and Jacob begins to justify his actions by describing a dream that he had had. In the dream, he saw that the he-goats mounting the females were striped and speckled and spotted, and an angel of God told him to take note of the dream and act accordingly. So you could say that Jacob was divinely guided in his plan. And yet he still had to follow through on the vision, to continue visualizing the spotted and speckled animals increasing, and to remain alert and observant.

Whether we know it or not, all day long we're creating sickness or health, prosperity or poverty. When you're about to take a risk, do you visualize or sense failure or success? Ask yourself whether or not you say, "See, I knew I would!" if you fail. Seeing something differently can shift your paradigm forever. That's why I say that healing requires creativity.

There's an earlier story from the Old Testament that illuminates this point clearly (Genesis 15:5–6). When Abraham is feeling down because he has no son and heir, God takes him outside and tells him, "Look up at the heavens and count the stars—if indeed you can count them." Then he says to Abraham, "So shall your offspring be." There's a play on words in the English translation that's obviously not in the original Hebrew but that I use to get the idea across: God tells Abraham in effect to "image a nation," which could be said as "imagination." God is trying to get Abraham to use his imagination to picture the potential for good that is in him. And that sparks something within Abraham, because the scripture says that he "believed the Lord, and he credited it to him as righteousness." Using his imagination, Abraham healed his own doubt in God, which could also be interpreted as doubt in his Higher Self, or in the Divine within.

4. Passion

There's a close bond between passion and purpose in life. As I just implied, my *purpose* may appear to be to heal people, but my real *passion* is to help people experience a loving God. Ideally, they would then learn to develop that relationship on their own so that they wouldn't need me anymore.

If you're having difficulty in life, especially in your career, you may come to the conclusion that you're not doing what you truly love. "But if I did do what I love," you reason, "I might not be able to make enough money at it to survive." Some years back, Marsha Sinetar wrote an empowering book called *Do What You Love, the Money Will Follow: Discovering Your Right Livelihood*. She never said that if you do what you love, you'll immediately get rich—or necessarily get rich at all. But she did say that you'd probably always have

can begin to see results. It doesn't have to be just the body; it can also be the life situations that are challenging you. You can learn to speak with the authority that's embedded within you, whether you're currently aware of it or not. The result may not be an instant cure of the ailment or situation, but it will be enough to motivate you to continue. (Later in the book, I'll show you how to use a form of prayer that you've probably never been taught in any religious organization, and it's based simply on speaking with authority.)

You need passion, and you need to understand the proper use of language to create results. Yet language on its own is no more helpful than passion alone. The apostle James asks in his Letter (2:14–26):

> *How does it help, my brothers, when someone who has never done a single good act claims to have faith? Will that faith bring salvation? If one of the brothers or one of the sisters is in need of clothes and has not enough food to live on, and one of you says to them, "I wish you well; keep yourself warm and eat plenty,"*

*without giving them these bare necessities of life,
then what good is that? In the same way faith: If
good deeds do not go with it, it is quite dead. . .
It is by my deeds that I will show you my faith.*

You can say that you have all of the faith in
the world that you're going to become a million-
aire someday or that you're going to be healed,
but if you don't do anything about it, nothing
will *ever* happen. You have to take action.

St. John of the Cross described the dark night
of the soul this way: When a boat has been
anchored in one spot for months without moving, it collects barnacles, and unless someone
comes along and scrapes off the barnacles, when
you push that boat out of its moorings, it's going
to be off center and may even capsize. The same
is true of our lives. The barnacles that cause us to
be out of balance are resentment, jealousy, anger,
greed, and gluttony. John says that we need to
learn how to bring the spirit of light into our
lives to get rid of those barnacles or, as Jesus
said, "something worse will befall you."

A healer or book can only jump-start you, but then you have to continue to maintain your life. Even if you were to be cured of diabetes today, if you don't practice the healing principles, in six months you could possibly discover that you have cancer.

5. *Language*

As I found out when I was having my stroke, it isn't always possible to use positive language when you're frightened or suffering. At the beginning of what appears to be a disturbing or painful experience, all sorts of negative thoughts and feelings may pour out of us, and it's better not to deny or attempt to repress them. When the stroke first began to set in, I was confused and subsequently became extremely angry and frightened. My staff allowed me to vent my powerful emotions of fear until I was able to hear what they were saying and let them care for me, get me to the hospital, and begin my own healing.

When people are venting their anger and fear, you don't need to tell them to stop. It's a little like the principle of witness consciousness in the Advaita Vedanta tradition of India, which teaches you to not judge your actions or mental shenanigans, but to observe them dispassionately. Often the very act of observation not only removes the emotional charge from potentially upsetting events, but it also tends to diminish negative thoughts—for it seems that those thoughts, like criminals who try to hide in the dark of night, don't like to be observed. In a similar sense, the Buddhist teacher Joan Halifax talks of just being present for someone who is suffering or dying. You don't necessarily have to do or say anything, she points out, but just be fully present for that person in a moment of anguish. And so, during my stroke, my partners Paul and Bruce were acting as healing agents by allowing me to express all of my fearful emotions without judging or reacting to them. They were witnessing for me, because in that moment of extreme fear, I wasn't able to step back and witness for myself.

Pay attention to the words you use, either spoken or in thought. Focus carefully on what you're actually saying: "I don't feel good today. I'm never going to make it through the day. Nothing appeals to me. Those people make me sick." This kind of language goes on for hours, and we're often unconscious of it. I certainly know what that's like—sometimes, worrying about a workshop can keep me up all night. But when I surrender to the moment and allow God to take over, I have all the energy I need. When I shift my awareness away from complaining to focusing on the power and aliveness that's in me, I usually end up giving the best workshop or seminar I've given in some time.

Don't sabotage yourself by expecting too much. We have to become more conscious of our dominant thoughts and recognize whether they're creating the energy of a positive or negative faith. When you become aware that you're creating negative faith, don't judge yourself, but observe what's happening. Try to take a few moments to come up with a positive thought to change the direction, and then sit for ten minutes meditating on that thought. I realize how impatient I can get with myself, and if I drop something, I may yell, "You idiot! How could you do that?" Now I realize what I'm doing, so I sit down and say to myself, "I'm not an idiot. I'm a Divine being." Just sitting with that thought changes my whole attitude.

Meditation is like eating food that then metabolizes into energy—which allows us to carry on with our lives and to work and communicate with others. The same goes for our thoughts. If we consume negative thoughts, our psychic and spiritual energy will be low or unreliable. In conflict resolution, counselors have long stressed the value of taking a "time-out" to let negative thoughts and violent emotions subside so that the warring parties can resume discussion on an even keel. In just that way, we may need to take a time-out with ourselves and feed ourselves some nutritious thoughts. Once we recognize that we're Divine, improvements tend to happen immediately.

Merely energizing positive beliefs isn't enough to keep us motivated, however. Without developing meaningful connections to other people, we'll have a hard time maintaining our passion and enthusiasm. People come to churches, synagogues, mosques, or temples for only one reason—relationships. It's not about doctrine; if the organization doesn't offer relationships, the people will leave. We wouldn't need 12-Step programs if religious organizations were doing what their founders intended, which is to lift up the downtrodden, heal the brokenhearted, and be there for one another. After all, no one heals alone. We need honest relationships that cultivate joy and laughter. Even the great mystics who have spent long periods of time in solitary meditation have done their greatest work by assisting other people up the mountain. Quiet times are essential for all of us, but their purpose is to achieve realization of oneness with God—oneness that then manifests as service.

I know, for instance, that I could not have healed from my stroke by myself. And I'm not referring only to the gifted doctors, nurses, physical therapists, and counselors who are all part of the medical establishment. I did need their talent and support, to be sure. But without my associates, the thousands who prayed for me, and the spiritual relationship that apparently developed between myself and Dr. Almeida, I never would have survived. That's an example of the kind of balance that leads to the healing that I discussed earlier.

6. Gratitude

It's easy to be thankful for health and abundance, but you must also learn to be grateful even when things go badly. As with fear and anxiety, it's difficult to feel grateful at the first onset of serious illness, which is often accompanied by pain and suffering. Gratitude is the opposite of self-pity—even today I can still fall into the "self-pity trap" if I'm not careful. It doesn't last as long as it once did, because I've learned how to get it out of my system quickly. But when you shift from self-pity to gratitude—taking stock of everything that has been a blessing—the low-voltage energy within you will immediately be raised to high-voltage.

The best way to do that is to develop an attitude of gratitude on a regular basis so that it becomes second nature. It's helpful to find at least one thing to be grateful for at the end of each day. While I was recovering from my stroke, for example, I was constantly given new exercises in physical therapy, and each one seemed more arduous than the last. It was challenging, yet just having people cheering me on made me feel lucky. I didn't feel grateful at first, but as I realized that all those people were helping to make *my* life better, I thanked them, and I thanked God for showing me a way to change. Sometimes it's just a matter of seeing everyday things in a new light. Try to imagine seeing things as God might see them, and this will help you to see yourself as Divine.

7. *Forgiveness*

You need to release the negative energy that keeps you from moving forward. To forgive isn't to condone another person's abusive or destructive behavior. Forgiveness is accepting that behavior as what it is, and then releasing it into the light. The Hebrew word for *forgiveness* translates to "drop it," and that's what you need to do: Release a hurt from the past or a person who has hurt you so that you can make your life whole. If you can do that, you may discover that some physical pain associated with your attachment to that hurt will also dissolve.

A woman named Peggy came to one of my healing intensives with a heavy burden that she had carried for years: She found it impossible to forgive her stepmother. Her biological mother had died while Peggy was very young, and her father remarried four years later. Peggy had three older brothers, but she was the only girl, and her stepmother was extremely abusive verbally and emotionally toward her.

"I can remember twice in my life when her abuse was so bad that I was sure I was going to die," Peggy said. "I ended up curled up in a corner just barely able to hold on to life. There was only one tiny spark left inside of me, and I could hear it saying in a little voice, 'She's killing me, she's killing me.'"

Peggy spent years in therapy of different sorts, including a course of Rolfing, but she was never able to get rid of the trauma she had suffered. That trauma had also begun to manifest as pain in her back in an area she came to call her "back-heart chakra," and it continued for many years along with her anger and confusion.

"I had to finally acknowledge that I actually hated my stepmother," Peggy said. "This affected my life in many ways. For instance, because of my hatred for my stepmother, I felt unworthy to be a Lector or Eucharistic Minister in my church. We were all taught the Commandment to honor your mother and father, and I hated her, which meant that I was breaking a Commandment."

During the healing service, we sang a song that includes the lyrics:

How could anyone ever tell you
You were anything less than beautiful?

How could anyone ever tell you
You were less than whole?
How could anyone fail to notice
That your loving is a miracle?
How deeply you're connected to my soul.

Peggy began to cry as her painful memories came up again. At that point, I said to the audience, "I want you to bring into your vision the person that you hate the most." In Peggy's mind, there was only one person she had ever hated at all, and that was her stepmom. But as I spoke those words, all she could think was, *Don't make me go there, Ron. I absolutely do not want to go there.* But then something relaxed and she was finally able to acknowledge her feelings of hatred.

"I brought her into my vision and I sang that song to her as we were directed to," Peggy said later. "As I sang to her and visualized her, I could see some of the things that had happened to her when she was little. I told her, 'I'm really sorry that those things happened to you. I hope that someday you and I can get along. All I've ever really wanted from you is for us to get along and for you to be my mom because you're the only mom I've ever had.' In my mind, she looked back at me and smiled, and all at once, the hatred was gone."

Peggy reported that the pain in her "back-heart chakra," which had been there for years, was also gone. "It just feels so good to have that horrible feeling gone, along with the sense that I was less than perfect because I hated this lady. I feel so blessed to be a free woman now."

If you run into a person who hurt you 20 or 30 years ago, and you're still carrying that hurt around but that person is having a great time, that probably makes you twice as angry. This means that you're only harming yourself: After all, whenever you point the finger at someone, three other fingers on your hand are pointing back at you. Holding a grudge enhances the negative energy that's already in you. But if, like Peggy, you can see the pain in the other person that caused them to hurt you, you may be able to find a way to forgive, and so begin your own healing.

❧

You can use each of these seven components to reconfigure your own personal programming as a first step to reclaiming your spiritual power. I call this the "healing of the subconscious mind." And don't think that just because you weren't raised with a set of dogmatic religious beliefs, you've somehow escaped programming. You could have had the most open-minded, nonjudgmental, loving parents in the world, and it doesn't matter—you've still been programmed. Countless things have been fed into your subconscious mind since the moment you were manifested into the world of matter, even in the womb.

You probably began to examine your programming when you were still in school. When you entered your rebellious adolescent stage, you may have questioned authority, beginning with what seemed like the arbitrary authority your parents exerted over you. You may have also questioned their religious beliefs, political convictions, or ideas about social status, art, music, and taste in clothing. Later you may have questioned the philosophical premises and economic principles on which society is based. As you moved deeper within, you probably began to examine your psychological programming, perhaps by entering therapy or reading about psychology. Maybe you realized, for example, that what seemed like inexplicable fits of rage or depression could actually be traced to how you were raised and how your parents treated you—and even how their parents treated them. Some behavior implanted within you on the subconscious level 30 or 40 years ago may be determining how you respond to certain situations today.

That raises the question of where God's responsibility ends and ours begins, of how much of our life is determined by fate and how much by free will. In his Letter to the Ephesians, Paul says "You must root out that rage from your life." He was telling his congregation that God wouldn't do everything for them; the responsibility to take back their own spiritual power was theirs. To reclaim your power without knowing you have the authority to use it is pointless, because you'll only lose it again. To have power, you must know that you have the authority, the confidence, and the self-esteem to act on it. If you're a victim, or if you see yourself as a victim of anything or anyone whatsoever, please get over it. You can't keep giving your power away to others—part of your responsibility is to take it back. You can do this by saying, "I'm not going to be a victim, and I'm not going to let you make me one."

Take Action

Now that you're familiar with the seven components of empowerment, you're ready to take action, which is the final stage of empowerment. None of what I've just said means anything until it's put into action. It's like tuning your engine perfectly and filling the tank with high-octane gasoline; but when you start your car, you just sit there admiring the hum of the motor without ever going anywhere. If you never leave your driveway, what's the point of owning a wonderful automobile?

In order to get moving, however, you first need to overcome your fear. Hunches, thoughts, and intuitive ideas come to you seemingly from out of nowhere, and may even fill you with an inkling of joy—but then the fear jumps up because there are always tapes playing in your mind: "You can't do that. No one in our family has ever done that. Why can't you be more like your sister? Why can't you compromise and clean up your act? It was good enough for your father!" Those thoughts come from the subconscious in a millisecond, so fast that you may be unaware of them unless you've learned to pay attention. All of these tapes have one purpose—to induce fear in you so that you won't go against the grain. If you ever hope to put those positive hunches into action, you'll have to overcome the fears that those tapes continue to generate in you. And one of the best ways to do that is through understanding authentic prayer.

Chapter Three

∽ ∾

Claiming the Power of Authentic Prayer

*A*uthentic prayer not only helps you overcome the fear that holds you back, but at
the same time, it helps you expand the
components of empowerment. That's because
authentic prayer, as I define it, is nothing less
than communion with the Divine Self of your
nature. Since that Self is essentially fearless, the
closer you come in contact with it, the more fearless you, in turn, become. The result is a syner-
gistic boosting of energy on all levels.

You may be wondering how to establish a
connection with part of yourself that can seem

foreign or unfamiliar at first. Here's an example of how this can work. Imagine that you've lost an item you cherish. Your first instinct is probably to run around the house and look everywhere for it. You don't immediately find your lost item, but in your search, you find yourself vacuuming the floor, doing the dishes, or cleaning the house . . . things that you'd been meaning to do but hadn't found the time for. So, as you're busy cleaning the house, that thing you were looking for pops up in the bottom of a drawer or under the bed— even though you had forgotten about it while you were occupied with other tasks.

In the same way, the answers you're hoping for in life can sometimes come from deep inside while you're looking for them "out there." You have to learn to be in the present moment, without the static of all of your negative beliefs and thoughts and the unfavorable projections of others. Only then will you be able to contact your Divine inner nature—a part of you that was there all along, but neglected because you hadn't found the time for it.

∽

Is authentic prayer about folding your hands? Maybe, if that helps you communicate better. Is it about kneeling on the floor? It can be, if that helps you feel a sense of awe. Is it about sitting and communing? Sure, if that makes you comfortable. But authentic prayer doesn't necessarily rely on any of those things. It's primarily about connecting with the Divine, and doing whatever you need to allow that to happen. This is all part of the inspiration that leads to real prayer.

Inspiration means activating the Spirit within. Once I watched a group of people doing tai chi, the Chinese martial art that's based on the natural movements of birds and animals. As I observed, I began to ask myself how the people who developed tai chi received the revelation that certain movements could be connected with the rhythms of nature. I had much the same thought while listening to Mozart one day a few years ago.

Don Campbell, author of *The Mozart Effect: Tapping the Power of Music to Heal the Body, Strengthen the Mind, and Unlock the Creative Spirit*, has a theory that listening to certain music, especially Mozart, can increase your clarity of intellect and sense of tranquillity, and can even help to heal certain imbalances in your health. As the music played, I found my body starting to move along with it. I hadn't planned on this, so I just got up and allowed the Spirit within me to start manifesting outwardly. I imagined that Mozart also must have been able somehow to connect with the pulse of life and the rhythm of the ocean, and he also moved with it.

While I was recuperating from my stroke, I asked friends to bring me CDs of Mozart, Rossini, and Vivaldi; listening to them, I felt connected to God. This divinely inspired music, along with scented aromatherapy candles and those "environmental fountains" that create peaceful sounds of flowing water, became a kind of conduit that helped me enter a sacred space. All of this enabled prayer to flow more readily.

Making a connection with Divinity on more than one level helps me enormously—the way some people like to set the stage for a night of romance with candlelight and sweet music—I see it all as filled with God. Once I've made myself aware of my Divinity, it helps me to have a conscious connection with the Divine, which is itself the nature of authentic prayer. Whether it leads to actual verbal prayer or not is almost secondary at that point. It may manifest as singing, chanting mantras, speaking in tongues, or just remaining silent and sensing the energy within what mystics call "the subtle body." Whatever form it takes, you know that you've made a connection with something that's stronger than your physical energy, and that knowledge increases the flow of Spirit within, which can then result in the healing of different levels of your being.

If the purpose of prayer is to make a connection to God, then this stage-setting is once again a form of prayer. Prayer isn't necessarily about healing or being healed per se, it's about making that connection with the Divine, which then heals you and others as a result. Have you ever been sick and had an inspiration to do something unusual to get a healing? Maybe it was to go to a practitioner outside of the allopathic field of medicine, such as an acupuncturist; cranial-sacral therapist; hypnotist; or some other complementary medical modality. Everything can be a grace and a gift, and if your hunch is to use it, you should, as Lorraine's story will show.

Lorraine's Hunch

A woman named Lorraine runs a shelter for abused children (from newborns through eight-year-olds) in the hills of Altadena, California. She diagnoses their needs and works with the families of these kids to get them back home or into foster care. One day she was approached by Clara, a woman who works with disabled mothers whose children are at risk due to their mothers' disabilities. One of Clara's "mothers" had just given birth to a set of twins, and Clara was concerned because the mother had bonded with her little boy but seemed to be rejecting the baby girl, who was diagnosed with Down syndrome and a cleft palate. The mother was saying things like, "I hate baby Sally," and Clara wanted Lorraine to see what she could do for the infant.

As a result of her cleft palate, Sally had almost no sucking reflex. It took several hours for someone to feed her even half an ounce of milk since she couldn't suck, and they had to put the milk in her throat drop by drop, like a baby bird.

"I thought that if Sally went to a foster mom who wasn't well trained," Lorraine says today, "she would die because she wouldn't get enough nutrition."

So when the twins were just a few weeks old, Lorraine accepted Sally and began to work with her. Lorraine had learned a simple healing practice at one of my intensives. We take a few deep breaths and whisper the words, "Come, Holy Spirit," inviting the Spirit of God to do Its healing work. We don't ask for anything at all, but rather issue the invitation and then wait for a response in whatever form it might take, allowing the Holy Spirit to do what It desires.

"I sat on a chair, took a bottle, and started to feed her," Lorraine later told me. "I looked her fully in the face and my first thought was, *Oh my goodness, she's not in there. Her spirit hasn't come into her body.* So I said, 'Come, Holy Spirit, come into baby Sally.' Then I spoke directly to Sally and said, 'You came into this lifetime to have the experience of Down syndrome and the mother you had, so please come in.'

"All of a sudden, the baby was in her body and she focused on my face and almost started to smile at me and become animated. Before, it had been like looking into an empty shell, but when she came into her body, she suddenly seemed so alive. 'Oh, Sally,' I said, 'you're such a beautiful little girl!' And when I said that, she smiled and started trying to suck on the bottle. I thought, *Oh, God, thank you, she's going to be okay.*"

Lorraine called Clara and said, "Don't worry, she's going to be fine. You can come and get her now."

About two weeks later, Lorraine received a call from Clara. "You're not going to believe this,"

Clara said. "The twins just went for their 30-day checkup, and the cleft palate on little Sally has disappeared. It just isn't there anymore." The cleft palate had been so obvious that the doctor was astonished. Even the characteristic features of Down syndrome that Sally had had were almost gone. The doctor ordered chromosome tests because he no longer believed that she even had the birth defect.

"I know that the Holy Spirit is there for healings, and it isn't about me," Lorraine said. "I need to understand that it isn't about my ego. It doesn't matter if you're worthy—we're all God's children, we all have divine souls, and He loves all of us. I understand that now."

Lorraine had let herself be open and alert to the potential source of the infant's problems. And although it was an unusual insight, she followed her hunch with remarkable results.

Chapter Four

❧

Healing
and Balance

*T*he one thing that will most help you reclaim your spiritual power is avoiding formulas and formulaic thinking. Formulas are fine for solving math problems or for figuring out the stress factors in steel beams, but they don't help very much when it comes to healing and prayer. In most cases, you would do better to follow a creative amalgam of common sense, intuition, and balance.

Take the everyday subject of nutrition. Most of us know that a reasonably balanced diet is the best way to achieve cardiovascular health and lower your chances of heart attack—or is it? I wouldn't be so brash as to say that we should just forget about following healthful dietary regimens; I follow one myself. But let's take a look at some of the other factors that may be involved with good health.

Can Lard and Wine Be Good for You?

In 1961, Stewart Wolf, M.D., then a professor at the University of Oklahoma School of Medicine, investigated Roseto, a town set in an area of eastern Pennsylvania amid the Poconos, where the rate of illness and death from heart disease was less than half the national average and nobody had ever had a heart attack before the age of 45. And yet, astonishingly, the men of the village all smoked cigarettes and drank wine aplenty. On top of that, most of the men worked 200 feet down in the earth in dangerous slate quarries nearby, while almost all of the women worked in local blouse factories with unhealthy conditions.

The people of Roseto favored traditional Italian meals, which were already bursting with cheese and sausage, and modified them with local ingredients that were the last word in toxic food. Although many dietitians recommend olive oil for cooking instead of animal fat, the poor immigrants who built Roseto as a self-contained community after being shunned by the English and Welsh populations in that part of Pennsylvania couldn't afford to import olive oil from Italy—so they cooked their sausages and meatballs in lard! What possible medical or dietary explanation could there be for these people's extraordinary good health?

Not surprisingly, it turns out that the healthiness of the citizens of Roseto had little to do with what they ate. What Dr. Wolf discovered was a tight-knit Italian-American community of fewer than 1,600 who lived in an atmosphere of mutual support and common interests in a way that seemed to protect its residents from the stresses of everyday life. In his book *The Roseto Story: An Anatomy of Health*, Dr. Wolf wrote about a world whose inhabitants tended to live in extended families in which grandparents, parents, and children dwelt in the same house in a system of mutual support and nurturance. "In the evening after supper, most families would walk around their neighborhood and chat and joke with each other," he said. "They were obviously enjoying each other's company." Rosetans also took active roles in more than 20 community organizations and civic groups, from the Italian social club to the PTA and Elks, and, as you might imagine, the Catholic Church. Dr. Wolf labeled the health benefits of living such a community style of life "the Roseto Effect."

What Dr. Wolf found in Roseto wasn't an isolated incident. A number of studies over the past 50 years have shown that people who are socially engaged tend to outlive those who aren't. Many studies have shown that married people live longer than those who are single, and that receiving personal support can lessen the effects of heart disease, increase the longevity of women with breast cancer, and help people recover from long-term addictions.

Certainly Roseto itself offers convincing proof of what happens when extended social and familial support dissipates, which has happened in most of the United States. In the early 1970s, younger people in the community began to work outside of the region, church attendance fell, and the pattern of three generations living in the same household began to disappear. In addition, economic and class differences pulled the social fabric further apart. Those who became more affluent began to socialize at an exclusive country club and moved away from the close-knit hub of town into larger, fenced-in spreads with expensive cars and more luxurious amenities. As the divisions widened, the health of the inhabitants declined to match the national average. And this was after much of the population had been persuaded to switch to a "healthier" diet!

The extended-family relationships that the people of Roseto enjoyed mirror the way I grew up. In my hometown, we never talked much about the relationship of food to being overweight or counted fat grams. I ate the same standard American diet that has been criticized for creating an epidemic of obesity in this country, and yet I never gained weight as long as I resided in that town. The women from my old neighborhood still live that way, socializing and interacting in ways that have all but disappeared elsewhere due to overwork and the fragmentation of families. And many of them are now in their 80s and 90s, probably eating in the same "unhealthy" way.

❧

Some years ago, *60 Minutes* ran a segment about what they called "the French Paradox": Although most French people ate large meals that generally included fatty foods, heavy sauces, and lots of butter and cream, their incidences of heart disease and serum cholesterol were less than half of Americans'. A theory was put forward that because the French also drink a lot of red wine with their meals, perhaps the presence of certain antioxidants in the grapes, such as resveratrol, had a healthful effect that more than compensated for all of that rich, fatty food.

A more significant part of the French Paradox, however, can be explained by the way that French eating habits have traditionally tended to relieve stress. We now know that stress causes the body to defend itself by secreting degenerative hormones and free radicals as waste products, both of which are now said to be the leading cause of cancer, heart disease, aging, and death. In France, as in other Mediterranean countries such as Spain and Italy, most people follow the patterns of traditional agrarian societies by making lunch the big meal of the day. In those countries, the midday meal can take two or three hours, often accompanied by wine and followed by a brief siesta—which is why not much business is done between 12 and 4 in that part of the world. The red wine does help by aiding digestion and overall relaxation and enjoyment, but the entire ritual is enhanced by a leisurely family setting. The satisfaction of such an enjoyable meal eaten in a relaxing environment goes a long way toward reducing stress and its debilitating con-sequences.

The opposite is just as true: If you get involved in an altercation at dinner with your kids or spouse, your digestion will most likely be disturbed and the food will turn toxic. It's not so much what we're eating in these cases, but what's eating us. There's more than a bit of truth in those scenes in the movies where someone pushes away from the table after an argument has flared up and says, "Now my dinner is ruined!" In a very real sense, that food has turned toxic, and it's better to stop eating altogether.

Rushing your meals by devouring fast food on the run, in the car, or while standing up can create similar toxic stress while diminishing the simple enjoyment of eating. Distracting yourself from the pleasure of mealtimes by watching TV, talking on the phone, opening mail, or having a "working lunch" at your desk not only depletes you emotionally but can interfere with digestion as well. Unfortunately, it turns out that the French have recently begun to eat more fast food, chips, and soda, and are now working through meals. As a result, their levels of obesity and heart disease have risen dramatically in the last ten years, especially among children.

Vietnamese Zen master Thich Nhat Hanh has made the point that much of our suffering comes from not eating mindfully. He says that smoking, drinking, and consuming toxins of all sorts actually causes us to consume our own lungs, liver, and heart. In his book *The Heart of the Buddha's Teaching: Transforming Suffering into Peace, Joy, and Liberation*, Hanh says that much of the despair, fear, or depression we experience may in fact be the residue of ingesting too many toxins, not only through unhealthful food, but also from watching violent films and television programs and playing certain kinds of computer and video games. He writes:

> *If we are mindful, we will know whether we are "ingesting" the toxins of fear, hatred and violence, or eating foods that encourage understanding, compassion, and the determination to help others. With the practice of*

mindfulness, we will know that hearing this, looking at that, or touching this, we feel light and peaceful, while hearing that, looking at this or that, we feel anxious, sad or depressed. As a result, we will know what to be in contact with and what to avoid. Our skin protects us from bacteria. Antibodies protect us from internal invaders. We have to use the equivalent aspects of our consciousness to protect us from unwholesome sense objects that can poison us.

The Importance of Being Balanced

For me, the Last Supper is the model for what all meals should be: a sacred expression of communion with those who share our table and, as a result, a sacred space to experience God. It's not enough to celebrate that famous supper at Mass or other religious services. We need to make *every* meal a sacred occasion and ingest only positive emotions along with good food. I'm not going to get into prescribing specific diets, but common sense and balance should prevail. For instance, if you eat meat, as most of us do, vary the source and don't just eat lots of highly marbled, fatty red meat. Most of all, eat reasonable portions; and balance your diet with fish, fruits, vegetables, and grains.

All life is about balance, but not always in the most obvious ways. Linda, a friend of mine who works as a film producer in Hollywood, was diagnosed with spots on her liver, which her doctors said might indicate cancer. The diagnosis stunned Linda because she had been eating a strict health-food diet and spending hundreds of dollars a month on vitamins and herbs.

When I was staying at Linda's beach house, she asked me to pray with her, and naturally I agreed. But first I had a practical suggestion that I didn't try to sugarcoat. "Why don't you go out and splurge once in a while?" I said. "Just eat something that you really want to eat. I'm not saying to have steak and lobster and banana cream pie every night, but follow your instinct to eat foods that give you pleasure."

I did some prayer work with Linda, and over time, she relaxed about her diet. When she went for her next checkup, much to her and her doctor's surprise, the spots had disappeared.

❧

Balance comes into play in healing in other ways as well, including how we integrate both allopathic and complementary medicine with divine assistance. There is a book in the Roman Catholic version of the Bible called "Ben Sira," or "Ben Sirach" (known as "Ecclesiasticus" in the Greek translation), that addresses this issue with great subtlety. Because Ben Sira was written about 200 years before Christ and after the time of Ezra (the person most responsible for redacting the Hebrew Bible into its present form), the book doesn't appear in either Hebrew or Protestant versions of the Bible, although it's in many scholarly versions. Ecclesiasticus is one of the so-called Wisdom books of the Bible, which offers a combination of worldly advice and spiritual admonition, and much of it is concerned with living a proper, moral life. However, in Chapter 38, the author, a wise Jerusalem scribe named Jesus Ben Sira, turns his attention to medicine and physicians:

Hold the physician in honor, for he is essential to you and God it was who established his profession. . . . From God, the physician has his wisdom and the king provides for his sustenance. His knowledge makes the physician distinguished and gives him access to those in authority. God makes the earth yield healing herbs which the prudent one should not neglect. Was not the water sweetened by a twig that men might learn its power, that is God's power? He endows men and women with the knowledge to glory in His mighty works, through which the physician eases pain and the pharmacist prepares his medicine.

Thus God's creative works continue without cease and the peace of God is all over the face of the earth. My child, when you are ill, do not delay but pray to God who will heal you. Offer your sweet smelling oblation and petition, a rich offering according to your means. Then give the physician his place, lest he leave, for you need him too. There are times that give him an advantage and he too beseeches God, that his diagnosis may be correct and his treatment bring about a cure.

Life is not either/or, Ben Sira is saying; it is both/and. So often we go from one extreme to the other—trying to heal by medicine without prayer, or by prayer without medicine. But it's necessary to utilize both and be creative and balanced in our approach to healing.

Chapter Five

❦❦

The Power
of the 23rd Psalm

Simply put, the 23rd Psalm is one of the most popular prayers in the Western world. It also happens to be one of the most powerful prayers ever uttered outside of the Lord's Prayer—which is partly based upon this Psalm. This beautiful collection of words can be the key to reclaiming spiritual power.

Most of us recognize the 23rd Psalm's familiar phrases, but what we don't often appreciate is the impact of the principles contained in the Psalm, probably because it doesn't fit the model of what we've been taught a prayer should be.

We believe that to pray means asking God to do something for ourselves or someone else. Psalm 23 is the recognition that everything we need has already been done; the writer of the Psalm is merely affirming that fact. As I noted before, Jesus never asked God to do anything to heal those he laid his hands on. Even in the Garden of Gethsemane, Jesus wasn't asking for anything; he was saying that he would do whatever was in God's will, even if it wasn't Jesus' own preference.

When I applied this realization to my own condition following my stroke, I had to ask myself, "Do I pray asking God to heal me of this stroke? Or do I just sit in the stillness and experience God?" Keep in mind that when Jesus said, "Seek first the kingdom, and all these things will be added to you," he was saying that God already knows our needs, and has responded to them before we ever ask. And so, I realized that I was no longer to pray for my own healing, but only to remember the covenant of humanity with God that's spelled out in the books of Leviticus and Deuteronomy in the Hebrew Bible: "You shall love the Lord your God, and you shall love your neighbor as yourself." After all, that's the line Jesus quoted when asked to boil the Commandments down to one thing.

If you keep that Commandment of love and compassion that's essential to the Divine covenant, as it says in Deuteronomy 28:1–8, then God will shower you with blessings: "You will be blessed in the town and blessed in the countryside; blessed, the offspring of your body, the yield of your soil, the yield of your livestock, the young of your cattle and the increase of your flocks; blessed, your basket and your kneading trough." And Proverbs 3:6 says that when you acknowledge God in all your ways, He will see that your paths are smooth. Those scriptures were among the first that impressed on me, more than 30 years ago, the need to be aware of the Presence of God in *everything,* even if you don't understand It. All of these thoughts started coming back to me in the first few weeks following my stroke. For, as the famous minister Kathryn Kuhlman used to say, "It's all there."

Here now is the text of the Psalm in a modern translation:

The Lord is my shepherd. I shall not lack. He makes me lie down in green pastures. He leads me beside the still and restful waters. He refreshes and restores my very life. He leads me in the path of uprightness. Yea, though I walk through the valley of the shadow of death, I will fear nor dread any evil, for you are with me. Your rod and your staff, they comfort me. You prepare a table before me in the presence of my enemy. You anoint my head with oil. My cup runs over. Surely only goodness, mercy, and unfailing love shall follow me all the days of my life. And through the length of days, I shall dwell in the house of the Lord forever.

Looking Deeper into the Psalm

If we examine the Psalm one phrase at a time, we begin to see not only its universal significance, but also the way in which it works as an affirmation of positive belief. This is implicit in the language, which is all in the affirmative mode. Let's take a closer look at each of the phrases in the 23rd Psalm.

The Lord is my shepherd.

You were probably taught to commune with the Divine by begging and pleading from a base of uncertainty. Yet this prayer doesn't begin, "The Lord is my shepherd, I think," or "The Lord is my shepherd, but only sometimes." It begins with an absolute knowledge through experience that the Divine principle will always guide us through all situations *without fail*. Whether or not King David wrote this Psalm, as tradition holds, its author certainly had the conviction that Divine guidance is always present.

I shall not lack.

The Zen master Rinzai, who lived in China in the ninth century, would hold up a finger to his students and ask, "What, in this moment, is lacking?" Perhaps his greatest interpreter, the 18th-century Japanese Zen master Hakuin, wrote, "At this moment, what more need we seek?" He also wrote,

"I say to you there is no Buddha, no Dharma, nothing to practice, nothing to prove. Just what are you seeking thus in highways and byways? Blind men! You're putting a head on top of the one you already have. What do you yourself lack?"

As this fiery Zen genius implied, we're constantly absorbed—obsessed even—with what's missing from our lives. It might be money, a place to live, the perfect partner, a fantastic physique, or a secure future. Ask yourself what you think you're lacking right now: Is it health? Prosperity? The right career? If you're praying authentically and living in the moment, you're not lacking anything. But if you feel that you're lacking, you're probably either living in the past or projecting into the future. By worrying about what isn't happening in the present moment, you declare your lack of confidence that the Divine is leading you exactly where you need to go. Whether you attribute such guidance to God, Atman, Buddha, Nature, the Universe, the Divine within, or simply to Being, once you surrender to Its power, you'll know for certain that you have nothing to fear, now or ever.

He makes me lie down in green pastures.

In our culture, green is the color of money, which probably isn't an accident, for that color is often symbolic of abundance and health. The Psalm clearly states that God desires that I live in abundance. God doesn't *ask* me to have abundance; He insists on it. We may do our best to scuttle His plans by sabotaging our best interests; engaging in defeatist thinking; embracing our low self-esteem; distracting ourselves with drugs, alcohol, wild living, or endless TV; or by ignoring the voice of our intuition that would lead us into spiritual and material well-being, but that doesn't alter the fact of God's positive intent for us.

He leads me beside the still and restful waters.

Water also has a symbolic history within most spiritual traditions. For instance, from the Great Flood and the drowning of the Pharaoh in the Red Sea to the baptism of Jesus in the River

Jordan, water has been integrally related to the Jewish and Christian religions. By the same token, the Quran speaks repeatedly of Paradise as a place of "gardens with streams of running water where [the good] will abide forever" (3:136), and Buddha referred to achieving enlightenment as crossing the river to "the far shore." These strong words shouldn't be surprising, for most of these civilizations held water to be a miraculous gift from God that can spell the difference between life and death.

"Still and restful waters" are distinguished from destructive flood waters, and they mirror the state of inner peace and tranquillity that authentic prayer requires so that you can hear the voice of God.

He refreshes and restores my very life.

By remaining open to the voice of God, which may come to you in the form of hunches, intuition, dreams, or chance encounters, your life will be enlivened at the center of your being. Divine energy in the form of *ch'i* (the Chinese and Sanskrit words for "vital energy" or "life force") flows into our systems constantly if we're attuned and make ourselves available to it. This energy revitalizes our bodies and our chakras, which are the centers of psychospiritual energy that regulate our physical, mental, and emotional activities.

He leads me in the path of uprightness.

The Noble Eightfold Path of the Buddha includes: (1) right views; (2) right intention; (3) right speech; (4) right action; (5) right livelihood; (6) right effort; (7) right mindfulness; and (8) right concentration. The idea is if you get all of those areas of your life right, then you'll be congruent and in harmony.

You don't have to be a Buddhist to understand the value of focusing mindfully on that sequence of "rights" (although Buddhists do have a very specific understanding of what each of them entails). A right understanding of the nature of life leads you to have the right intention, which is a dispassionate benevolence characterized by an aversion to harming others. If your intention is to cause no harm, then you'll use right speech—that is, you'll abstain from lying, slander, gossip, and other misuses of your verbal faculties that are hurtful to others. Consequently, you'll avoid wrongful actions as well, such as murder, stealing, and sexual misconduct. You'll also pursue a livelihood that doesn't harm anyone while also performing a needed service. Such an upright life would be difficult to maintain without a proper exercise of effort, a discipline to break the grip of habit. Mindfulness and concentration are two manifestations of meditation practice that help facilitate all forms of right living.

> **Yea, though I walk through the valley
> of the shadow of death, I will fear nor
> dread any evil, for you are with me.**

Death is an illusion, yet we're all afraid of it. Jesus said, "Do not resist evil." Since we tend to see death as evil, he might have said, "Do not resist death." Whenever you're faced with a painful situation, you have three options: (1) You can resist it, which means that you'll be in conflict, and therefore continue in pain; (2) you can try to change the situation, which may mean acting upon it directly or withdrawing yourself from it— whether the situation is a job you hate or a relationship that doesn't fulfill you; or (3) if you can't change or leave the situation, you can accept it as it is. Acceptance or surrender doesn't mean acknowledging that a given situation is right or good; it simply means that it is what it is at this moment. From that perspective, walking through the darkest ravine can't intimidate you, because it's one with the same Divine Reality that's within you.

Your rod and your staff, they comfort me.

The staff and the shepherd's crook have served as symbols of power and authority at least as far back as Egyptian times. This reference isn't to the authority of autocratic power, but rather to a sense of mastery. We say that athletes look comfortable making a great play, for they have the authority that comes from skill and self-confidence. In other words, they make it look easy. In the same way, when Jesus began his ministry, the Gospel of Mark says, "The people were amazed at his teaching, because he taught them as one who had authority, not as the teachers of the law."

Here, the writer of the Psalm is drawing strength from the authority of the Divine. The Latin verb *confortare* means to strengthen greatly—the root is *fortis,* strength—and that strength is at the base of genuine comfort.

You prepare a table before me in the presence of my enemy.

Your enemy doesn't have to be another person—it can be illness, fear of change, or an attitude of lack. But even in the midst of your fears, there's a table right in front of you that's overflowing with the joys and abundance of life. All you need to do is shift your frame of reference and focus on the profusion of opportunity that surrounds you.

You anoint my head with oil;
My cup runs over.

Oil was used in ancient times to anoint kings, and has been taken by many spiritual traditions as a symbol of the Divine Spirit that dwells within us, causing our lives to overflow with joy.

Surely only goodness, mercy, and unfailing
love shall follow me all the days of my life;
And through the length of days I shall dwell
in the house of the Lord forever.

This prayer is about living in the consciousness of the Divine. It's about the principles of blessing and decree, which is the technical term for bringing about, through your communion with the

Divine, something that you want to manifest. (We'll discuss the idea of decree further in the next chapter.) Psalm 23 isn't about faith, or even about belief, because faith and belief can sometimes be imbued with doubt. When you know something in your heart, you leave no room for doubt.

Psalm 23 is saying how important it is to become aware of our Divine nature. Once we do, we can affirm these truths as real because we've experienced them. They're part of our inheritance, which flows to us by virtue of having followed the covenant that God gave to humanity going back to Noah, Abraham, and Moses. In his book *The Jesus Code*, John Randolph Price deciphers that code to be, "I am as Jesus." That's all we need to know. The spiritual path isn't concerned with doing anything—its main objective is to become aware that we are of Spirit, which means that we are Divine. "God's being is my being," Meister Eckhart said. "Wherever I am, there is God." That realization opens up the kingdom within for the gifts and the fruit of the Spirit to flow out from us.

෫ඏ ඏ෫

Chapter Six

౨ ౭

Authentic Prayer by Decree

Sometimes language can constrict us as much as it frees us. When I speak of prayer and use words such as "command" or "decree," it's difficult to avoid the negative associations that these terms have with respect to autocratic or dictatorial power. At the very least, such words leave us sounding like spoiled brats making outrageous demands. And yet, praying in this way can be very natural and assured; far from being imperious, it actually expresses faith in a power greater than oneself.

In the sacred writings of the Christian Testament (Mark 11:22–24), Jesus said:

Have faith in God. . . . I tell you the truth, if anyone says to this mountain, "Go, throw yourself into the sea," and does not doubt in his heart but believes that what he says will happen, it will be done for him. Therefore I tell you, whatever you ask for in prayer, believe that you have received it, and it will be yours.

When Jesus uttered those words, he was telling the people to have the faith that comes from realizing the Divine Spirit, the Source of all good, within. This is the faith that allows you to say something and know that before the words even leave your lips, it has already been taken care of. In that sense, when you speak to your mountain, you have the assurance that God had when (according to the Creation story in Genesis) He said, "Let there be. . . ." God actually spoke the earth and the oceans, the sun and the moon, and the plants and the animals into creation.

We tend to forget the presence of the power to create that resides in our own words. Perhaps that's because we're not fully aware of how our actions or results tend to follow our thoughts and speech. When we become aware of this process, we can pray in a way that's sometimes called "to decree"; when we do this, we speak from what we know to be truth, which is the Divinity of our own nature as children and heirs of God.

Jesus knew that he was God's child, but I wonder if *we* know this about ourselves. As God's child, Jesus knew what kind of spiritual power was at his disposal. Are we aware of this? At some point in his life, Jesus claimed his nature as being one with God's. Have we claimed that truth for ourselves yet? Jesus sought the guidance of God within his own being. Do we know to look there?

These questions raise the issue of how we can go about reclaiming our true nature as God's children, and by doing so, experience the spiritual power that flows from an understanding of authentic prayer as Jesus practiced it. We don't need to become Christians or join a church to have that understanding. Whatever our spiritual path, we can include and put Master Jesus' teachings into effect in our lives.

Integrating Our Human and Divine Selves

When crises occur, we can remain steadfast in our belief that we'll overcome the difficulty by being aware of our reclaimed spiritual nature—just as I did when I went to Brazil and watched Joao de Deus do his miraculous work. Once I was there, I rededicated myself to my original commitment of priestly service made some 30 years ago: to be of service to God and others by allowing God to manifest His glory through me by any means He chooses. Standing close to Joao while he performed visible surgeries without anesthetics made me deeply aware of his trust in God—and in the process, a trust I once had and have now recovered—for as the saying goes, "If God be for you, who can be against you?"

Joao doesn't place his trust in his intellectual capabilities, since he has had little formal education. Instead he places it in the veracity of the visions and guidance he's received to do God's work. Watching him made me realize that I had been that way myself in the first 25

years of my ministerial work, but I had somehow lost my focus. Now, since I've reclaimed my
spiritual inheritance and accepted my Divine
nature along with my human nature, that focus is
returning in abundance.

When I speak of my Divine nature, in no way
am I claiming to be God, but rather to be, like all
of God's children, an emanation of the Divine. As
Meister Eckhart once said, "God's seed is in us
and God's seed grows into God."

You can share in this awareness by saying to
yourself, "I am an individualized expression of the
Holy Spirit." Your true spiritual power will become
evident when you know the truth of that statement.

I believe that my stroke happened as a blessing, an underscoring of all of the spiritual truth I
had just experienced with Joao in Brazil. It was as
if the universe was saying, "Okay, now use what
you've relearned and reclaimed." As the Roman
theologian Tertullian wrote centuries ago, "Faith
without action is dead."

I haven't written this book as a healing book
per se—it's more about the glorious manifestation

of God's love that's available to us as our inheritance, regardless of our religious tradition. I don't teach the principles in this book so that you can learn how to go to God and get healing or anything else. The goal is to learn how to live as a spiritual being who wants for nothing, which has been God's intention since the dawn of time.

To know this truth is to be blessed, and when you are, you know it isn't just for yourself that you've received such blessings. Part of the gift you've received is for you to be a blessing to others, too. My fondest desire is that my words bless you, and you, in turn, bless others. The blessing I'm speaking of more often than not takes the form of prayer, and since I've been speaking about authentic prayer and decree, I'd like to give you a brief outline of what I believe defines real prayer.

1. **Prayer is a means to unite with God—** it's not a way to get something from God. When Jesus said "Seek first the kingdom of God," he meant to seek the

oneness of God in the present moment, and then everything else you need will flow from that.

2. **Prayer is a means to know God**—not knowing *about* God, but knowing and experiencing Him directly.

3. **Prayer is itself turning within,** and that's also the proper attitude to have while you pray.

4. **In prayer, we seek the nature of God.** This doesn't necessarily mean that we should seek to verify what we've been told about God; instead, we should discover the nature of God on our own. That's why meditation, which takes us deeply inside our own selves, is such an essential form of prayer.

5. **Prayer is an authentic, powerful communion with the Divine,** which means

allowing yourself to be in the presence of God without your mind working. In true communion with God, there's no need to ask for or tell anything; in fact, there's no need for any mental process whatsoever. In Jeremiah 33:3, God says, "Ask me anything and I will tell you secrets you have never known." Through meditating on this passage over many weeks, I came to understand that the ultimate prayer isn't what I do or think—it's what God reveals to me about Himself and all other subjects.

6. **Prayer is any attitude that helps you to receive God's grace,** to hear that "still small voice" of the Divine prompting, and to receive an inner assurance.

7. **Through prayer, we can open up the kingdom of God that's within us to flow outward.**

Letting Our Divinity Shine Through to Others

In some of my previous books, I've talked at length about the deeper meaning of the terms for *prayer* in Sanskrit and Aramaic, but now I'd like to add a new level of insight to what I've already said. The Sanskrit term for *prayer*, "pal al," means "seeing yourself as wondrously made," and it's true that we *are* wondrously made as physical beings, because the body-mind complex is one of the great miracles and mysteries of all creation. Even our greatest scientists, physicians, and psychologists can't explain exactly how the body and mind function. But the higher vibration comes from understanding that we're wondrously made as the individualized expression of the Holy Spirit. When Jesus said, "Don't hide your light under a basket," he was talking not just about our talents and abilities, but also about our spiritual nature. He was telling us to learn to let our inner Divinity shine through and be a beacon to others. It's not so much what we do on the material plane, but what God works through us if we just get out of His way. That's the light we're all hiding.

I've also talked about the Aramaic word for *prayer*, "slotha," which means "to set [your mind as] a trap" to catch the thoughts of God. Recently, I've come to see that prayer isn't about our words or thoughts—it's about the realization of oneness with God and all creation, brought about through a loving, listening ear and heart. Prayer isn't about the mouth; it's about the ear.

To fully understand prayer, I had to look at my teacher, Jesus, and ask myself if he ever prayed for anything material. Because if he did, then that would be the model I should follow. To determine whether he did, I had to restudy the four Gospels and disregard anyone else's word on this subject. And in the end, I found that Jesus never prayed for *anything* material—never once did he ask for goods of any sort, nor did he ever ask for healing. Instead, he was teaching people how to realize the presence of God. Jesus always encouraged people to pray for spiritual guidance, and he showed them that out of that prayer of realization would come the power to meet all of their needs. When he multiplied the loaves and fishes (Matthew 14:19–20), Jesus didn't ask God to increase the food: "Taking the five loaves and the two fish and looking up to heaven, he gave thanks and broke the loaves. Then he gave them to the disciples, and the disciples gave them to the people." Rather than beseech God for help, Jesus expressed gratitude and then let his disciples take over.

When Jesus met someone who was sick or in emotional or mental conflict, he simply declared that what appeared to be negative didn't exist, for he saw God as all good and everywhere present. That's all you need to be aware of when you pray by decree.

But can decreeing work in our time, when that kind of absolute certainty seems to be in short supply? Let's look at the following story for an example.

Susan, a woman who came to one of my workshops, wanted to heal her relationship with her father, who had died 13 years previously. At the time of his death, she thought that their relationship was better than it had been for a long time. But during the years since he died, Susan began to be aware that she couldn't forgive her father because of certain things that had happened in their relationship. Those hurts, and her inability to forgive them, were diminishing her self-esteem in other relationships and damaging her physical health as well.

At the workshop's healing intensive, Susan had declared her intention to heal her relationship with her father. "During lunch, someone brought to my attention that it was Rosh Hashanah, the Jewish New Year," she later said. "My father was Jewish, and I got chills, realizing what a propitious day this was for him and me to heal. So I took a little time to go in my room and get quiet, and I called for the presence of my father to be with me. I wanted to talk to him, and so I made a decree that our relationship was healed, including all the pain, hurt, anger—anything that was less than loving. I just said that any negative feelings that we had been holding between us during his life were healed and released, and that we're now both forgiven and free to be ourselves in this life and the next and to love each other as we always did in our hearts."

During the afternoon session, while I was in a meditative trance, Susan was called up on the stage and I wrote a note that was handed to her. The note said, "The unkindness you experienced with your father is healed. Be joyful." Since I was in trance, I obviously had nothing to do with the content of the note, but was just passing it along. Susan had decreed healing between her father and herself, and it happened just as she said.

Chapter Seven

୬ ୭

Meditations
and Prayers

I've already said that what you read here won't mean all that much unless and until you take some kind of action to put my words into practice. So, rather than close the book with the traditional epilogue or summation, I'd like to leave you with a series of spiritual exercises that can help you reclaim your spiritual power in a very direct way. Each of the exercises that follow offers another angle of approach, another doorway to realizing the presence of God. These exercises are focused on prayer and meditation (I've also included some healing practices in the Appendix).

❦

The best way I know to actively reclaim your spiritual power is to learn to keep yourself in the presence of the Divine as continually as possible. Bear in mind that all of the great traditions have practices that help you to focus on the present moment or develop an awareness of God. Many of these practices were originally developed by and for monks and mystics who devoted their lives to Divine realization. In the Catholic tradition, for instance, monks and nuns often used a form of meditation in which they would contemplate a passage of scripture or some mystical truth for long periods of time. Perhaps the best-known version of this practice is the "prayer of the heart" from Eastern Orthodox Christianity, where one calls on the name of Jesus repeatedly ("Lord Jesus Christ, Son of the living God, have mercy on me, a sinner"). I've created a variation on this practice that opens it up to people of all religious backgrounds.

Awareness of the Presence of God
(Contemplative Meditation)

This kind of contemplation is concerned with getting to a place where you're open enough to hear the still small voice of God within you. Be patient with yourself, for this may not happen right away.

The night before you begin, say to your-self, with the intention that you'll maintain an attitude of openness and attentiveness: "The kingdom of God is within me."

The next morning when you awake, take three deep breaths and bring that idea back into consciousness: "The kingdom of God is within me." Lie in bed and just listen and wait for several minutes. Don't be concerned if you don't hear any response or sense any intuition at first. I'm using the word hear *in a very broad sense, of course. You may hear all sorts of mind chatter, for instance, such as your log-ical brain telling you that this is foolish or*

*won't really work. You'll "hear" yourself plan-
ning dinner or going over the work you have to
do later. But after that subsides, you may hear
a question, such as, "What is the kingdom of
God?" You may also hear an affirmative answer:
"The kingdom is I." Or you could hear an inner
voice saying, "You're my beloved one." Of
course, you may not hear words at all; you may
instead sense a feeling of peace or joy. This feeling may seem to have nothing to do with
God—but the kingdom of God is really about a
relationship, so don't be concerned.*

*Five or ten times each day, take a minute
or two to recall that the Divine presence is
with you. Take three deep breaths and bring
that same thought into consciousness for
about two minutes. If you spontaneously find
yourself sitting for longer, that's fine, but
don't strain or push yourself. Just be calm and
recognize that God is the source of all your
good. This entire exercise is about nothing
other than developing a conscious awareness
of the presence of God.*

As you go down to breakfast, stop and repeat the process. As you leave for work or get into the car to run errands, stop for a minute before you turn the key in the ignition, and again call into consciousness the awareness that God is within you. You're never in such a rush that you can't spare 15 seconds to call yourself back to awareness. Do this practice again during your lunch break, while sitting at your desk in the afternoon, and while driving home from work. Prior to going to sleep at night, take a little longer, as you did in the morning, to express thanks for the assurance of the presence of that Spirit within.

That's all there is to it.

There are plenty of books about meditation on the market if you'd like to begin or deepen your practice. Some are oriented to particular traditions, such as Buddhist, Christian, Jewish, or Sufi meditation. But the most useful book on the subject that I've come across is *The Best Guide to Meditation*, by Victor N. Davich. It explains the basic principles of meditation in most of the world's traditions and then offers a simple way to begin a regular practice, and it doesn't use jargon or foreign terminology. I recommend working with this or other books to develop a facility with meditation that will assist you in many of the exercises described here.

God's Radiation Therapy
(Healing Meditation)

When I lead healing services or workshops, I like to leave everyone with a practice they can take home and use themselves. It's a simple practice I call "God's Radiation Therapy." It consists entirely of laying hands on yourself or another individual for five or ten minutes in total silence. Think *I am God breathed* three times, then place your hands on whatever part of the body needs healing and remain quiet. Allow the Divine essence in your being to move through your arms and engulf you (or the other person) with radiant light. You can also show a close friend or loved one how to do this for you. For example, if your difficulty is in your shoulder, have someone put their hands on your shoulder, wherever they're guided, and keep quiet. Most people think they need to pray or say some comforting words, especially if they belong to a religious denomination, but silence is actually a more effective medium for healing in this exercise.

Try this every morning for ten minutes for one week.

∽

Speaking to Your Mountain
(Healing Meditation)

In her autobiography, Myrtle Fillmore, co-founder of the Unity School of Christianity, talked about the time when her body was decaying and her organs were beginning to fail. One day in meditation, however, she realized that she could speak to her body and get results. Because of her advanced state of deterioration, she had to speak to her body every day for several months, but the desired results still came. This is what Jesus meant when he referred to "speaking to your mountain": You have an energy within you that can help you heal if you learn to gain access to it, but you have to practice. The first thing you need to do is understand that you have this kind of authority. Any- and everything that the enlightened masters of the world possessed, you already have within yourself. The only difference between Jesus, Yogananda, Sai Baba, and the rest of us is that they *knew* they were Divine, and we don't.

To say you're a Divine being doesn't mean that you think you're God and therefore don't have to answer to anyone. Think of this example: When you go outside on a beautiful sunny day, you can't enjoy the sun by looking directly at it or you'll damage your eyes. But if you turn your back on the sun and look at the rays of sunlight as they bounce off the water, the flowers, or a windowpane, you'll feel delight. Although that brilliant light and color isn't the sun itself but an emanation of it, it's still powerful. That's how it is with you and me: We come from this great ball of pure, Divine light, and we reflect it.

For this meditation, you're going to take Jesus' concept of speaking to your mountain, filtered through the way Myrtle Fillmore used it and the way I have applied it to myself. Some years ago, I was in San Simeon, California, and I discovered a lump growing under my arm. It frightened me because I didn't know exactly what it was. Over a period of two days, it grew larger, until it was about half the size of a hardboiled egg and almost as hard. When I realized how large it had become in such a short time, I started to panic. But after a while, I calmed myself as best I could and waited for guidance.

The ancient Aramaic word for *prayer*, as I've already noted, means "to set a trap," and in that sense, I set my mind to catch the thoughts of God. Very shortly, I heard a voice within me say, "Just put your hand on the lump and think only God, and be quiet for the next 30 minutes." It's not so easy to keep your hand in one place for 30 minutes. The first five or ten minutes I was extremely restless, especially after the state of near-panic I had been in previously. But after ten minutes or so, I began to feel the restlessness and tension decreasing, along with my fear, and then I slowly felt an emanation of energy welling up within me.

After about 30 minutes, I put my hand down and felt something inside of me say, "It's done. Go about your day." I paid no more attention to it for the rest of the day. In the evening, I put my hand up to feel the swelling and noticed that it was half the size it had been in the morning. Not only had it stopped growing, but it had reversed itself. When I mentally asked myself what I should do, I got the same message: "Do it again." I did, and this time it was much easier. The half hour seemed to fly by, and I went to sleep feeling calm and centered. When I got up the next morning, it was about the size of a pea. By the evening of the second day, it was completely gone. I had done nothing more than sit in the stillness.

These days, when I deal with tumors and

cancers in other people, we don't sit in the silence. I speak to that mountain as if it were the mountain in front of me, and I remove it—and you can, too, with practice. Depending on the receptivity of each individual, the person may be healed 30 percent, 70 percent, or even 100 percent. The determining factor is our combined level of belief. We begin with God's belief system (if you want to call it that), then you factor in my belief system and the subject's belief system. We can count on God 100 percent, but the level of belief in you or me may fluctuate on any given day. All I can do is show you how I learned to do this to myself—your belief will make all the difference.

Take a couple of deep breaths and get as relaxed as possible. Choose a position in which you feel comfortable, whether it's sitting on the floor or in a chair, or even lying down. Meditation teachers advise against lying down during meditation because of the tendency to fall asleep, but this isn't that kind of meditation. The effectiveness of healing prayer doesn't depend on your posture, but on how relaxed you are.

During this exercise, you'll speak to your entire body methodically, covering a wide range of potential trouble spots. I recommend following the complete routine. Of course, if you need healing in a particular area of your body, you may want to spend more time speaking to that area. The way to speak to your particular mountain is to address whatever is impeding your flow of energy and preventing you from living fully.

You should repeat each of the following phrases at least once.

To the liver, the kidneys, and the pancreas, speak these words: "You are full of vigor, full of energy, full of vitality."

To your heart, say: "The pure love of Divine Spirit flows in and out through your wonderful, joyous pulsations."

To the stomach, spleen, and abdomen, say: "You are energetic, strong, and intelligent, no longer infected with negative ideas of disease placed there by myself or medical doctors."

Then stop, take a deep breath, and affirm that your entire body is filled with the energy of God. Sit in silence for a moment and then move on to your limbs.

Say to your arms: "You are active and strong, with no pain anywhere. Blood flows to you without any hindrance." After you repeat that, say the same thing to your hands, legs, and feet in succession.

Next, speak to your eyes: "You express the sight of the Holy Spirit drawing on an unlimited source of power. You are young, clear, bright eyes because the light of God shines through you."

To your brain, say, "You are filled with light. The thoughts emanating from you are lucid and coherent."

To your lungs, say, "You are filled with the light of health. There is no darkness or undue fluid within you."

Then speak to your body as a whole: "Body, forgive me for the foolish, ignorant course that I pursued in the past when I condemned you as weak, inefficient, and diseased.

I will not be discouraged but will speak to you, my body, with hope, knowing that in due time you will respond to my words of power and authority and will heal totally. I thank you, God, for the realization of this Divine truth."

Take a deep breath and sit in the quiet for a few moments. Then affirm this truth within your belief system: "I love my body. My body loves to be healthy. My heart is the center of love. My blood has life and vitality flowing in it. Every cell of my body is filled with light energy. I am healthier now than I have ever been. I appreciate my glorious body."

Finally, take a deep breath and express your gratitude in any way that's comfortable for you in silence. Take another deep breath and open up your eyes.

ᕗ

The Healing Heart
(Healing Prayer)

This is a powerful practice for direct self-healing. It's simple, straightforward, and utilizes a high level of faith. If you feel comfortable doing this, put your hand on the area where you're experiencing problems. If you have knee problems, difficulty thinking clearly, trouble with your hearing, or a bad back, just place your hand on those parts of your body. But I've also found that healing happens just as effectively if you place the hand on the area that corresponds to the heart chakra, which is the center of the chest and the center of the whole system of psychospiritual energy that regulates your body and soul. It covers the whole aspect of your being, thoughts, body, will, and emotions.

Take a deep breath and speak the following out loud, whether you're alone or in a group:

"I feel the presence of the Divine. I feel the power of God's energy moving through me now, healing and restoring me. I feel an exuberance, an enthusiasm, an exhilaration that makes me aware of the Divine presence that is always with me, in me, and flowing from me. I'm grateful for this healing. I'm grateful for the presence of peace. I'm grateful

*for being made aware that God loves me. All is well
in my world. I'm at peace and I'm grateful. Amen."*

Take a deep breath, relax, and be grateful.

∽

"I Am God Breathed"
(Healing Prayer)

I've presented this exercise in previous
books, but I repeat it here because it is such a
linchpin for all the healing work I do. If you
accept that the prerequisite for healing is a
heightened awareness that God dwells within
you, and so, offers you the opportunity to heal
yourself, then this exercise brings that awareness home to roost.

Close your eyes for a few moments and take
three deep breaths. On the inhale, bring into consciousness the words *I am*, and on the exhale, *God
breathed*. You'll be silently chanting *I am God
breathed*. Do that three times at the beginning of
each meditation, and then just breathe normally.
If you're comfortable closing your eyes, feel free

to do that. If you'd rather sit on the floor or even lie down, do whatever is comfortable for you. Next, speak the following out loud:

"Divine Spirit, we welcome you. You are the healing presence of our heavenly Father/Mother, that healing presence of boundless, never-ending love that restores, heals, and transforms. Divine Spirit, we call you forth from the essence of our being, and in this present moment, we realize your unlimited love for each of us. In that awareness alone, the healing energy of your love is released and, in this present moment, begins to transform and heal our lives. And for this we are grateful. Amen."

Honoring the Light
(Ceremonial Prayer)

The following ritual is taken from the Jewish Haggadah, a short book that's read aloud each year at the Seder, the festive meal celebrating the beginning of Passover and commemorating the escape of the Jews from Egyptian bondage. During the ritual, members of the community light candles and ask God's healing for family, friends, relatives, and neighbors.

Some parts of the Haggadah quote the Torah, some were written as long ago as 2,000 years, and others date from the Middle Ages. More than 2,700 editions have been produced, including many modern revisions such as the one below. While respecting the sanctity of the ritual celebration of Passover, I believe that the sentiments in the Haggadah can be seen as universal. This is an exercise ideally celebrated with a group.

Place candles on a table, home altar, or central area in the home or meeting place. Each participant should come up and light a candle while the following prayer is recited aloud by all.

"We begin by honoring the light. We light these candles for our families, loved ones, friends, and all of our relations. We light them for those who are near and for those from whom we feel an unwanted distance; for the newborn,

the elderly, and all the wounded children. May the candles inspire us to use our powers to heal and not to harm, to help and not to hinder, to bless and not to curse. May the radiance pour out upon our hearts and spread light into the darkened corners of our world."[1]

---

[1] Adapted from *A Passover Haggadah* by Rachel Altman and Mary Jane Ryan.

Appendix

Daily Healing Practices

෴

*H*ealing is an ongoing process, rather than a one-shot deal. We all need to be more aware of what we're doing on a minute-by-minute basis. Remember the story of Nan-in and Tenno from the Introduction, and be alert to even the small things you do, such as where you place your umbrella—or your unkind thoughts. Try to focus on being positive and staying in the present moment. To help you with this process, I put together a series of passages taken from the sacred scriptures of the world's religions. Each quotation is followed by a reflection on the meaning of those words. I then created a brief prayer based on the scripture and the reflection, followed by an appropriate positive affirmation and an action step. These are just different ways of looking at the same idea, much like holding a prism up to the sun and letting the white light filter through and break into an array of different colors.

But, as I said earlier, none of that means much until the ideas, reflections, and affirmations urge you to take action. The whole point is to change your level of awareness. Work with each excerpted scripture, reflection, prayer, affirmation, and action step for a day (or even up to a week) before moving on to the next one. And after you get the knack of these exercises, you can begin to create similar ones of your own.

HEALING PRACTICE #1

- **Sacred Scripture:** *Islam—Quran 72:13.* "Anyone who believes in his Lord has no fear."

- **Reflection:** O God, since I was a child, I have been taught to fear You. It was instilled in me since early on that You were out to get me. This is one of the reasons that I have been incapable of having an intimate relationship with You. In fact, many of my fears affect my other relationships in a negative way. How can I get over this hurdle?

- **Prayer:** God, I know with my *head* that You are my Divine Mother and Father, but I want to know this truth in my *heart*. That way, I can begin to deal with my fears fearlessly.

- **Affirmation:** God is my peace, and I walk daily in the knowledge that God is *for* me, not against me.

- **Action Step:** Observe your fears and choose one to deal with today. For example, if you're fearful of expressing yourself in certain situations—maybe at work or in a relationship— express your opinions lovingly, but firmly, in at least one such instance today.

HEALING PRACTICE #2

- **Sacred Scripture:** *Judaism—Nehemiah 8:10.* "The joy of the Lord is my strength."

- **Reflection:** Funny, I never would have associated strength with joy. But there is an energy in joy that does uplift and strengthen me. Lately, however, I have forgotten how to laugh and have a good time. I have also noticed how drained I feel, and it is important for me to get back to enjoying life. But how?

- **Prayer:** God, it is my greatest wish to celebrate life and be fully alive again. I need a spirit transfusion: My drooping spirit needs to be replaced by Your joyous Spirit. Come, Spirit of God, enliven me with Your presence.

- **Affirmation:** Every atom of my body is being energized by God's Spirit, and I am feeling revitalized.

- **Action Step:** Today, decide to do something that you enjoy, makes you happy, and fills you with laughter. It might be a telephone call to a friend who knows how to transcend life's challenges and bring others a sense of joy; or it might be jumping into some leaves during autumn, as you did when you were a child— you decide! But do it now.

HEALING PRACTICE #3

- **Sacred Scripture:** *Christianity—John 5:2-6.* Jesus went to Bethesda (a pool near the sheep-gate) where there were many people who were sick—some were blind, some crippled, and some paralyzed. One man had a lingering disease of 38 years' duration. Jesus went up to him and asked, "Do you want to be whole?"

- **Reflection:** I don't think I have any idea what wholeness could possibly feel like. What could it entail? Does it mean that the body is perfectly healthy? Does it mean that one thinks only positive thoughts? Or does it have to do only with spiritual things, since Jesus was the one who asked the question? Am I somehow supposed to integrate my entire body, mind, and spirit? How?

- **Prayer:** God, I want to feel whole, but I'm not sure how that feels. Help me by guiding me in understanding the experience of wholeness. I know the master Jesus was whole, but I still don't know *how* he was whole. Lead me, guide me, for I truly desire to be whole.

- **Affirmation:** I am born of God and I am alive, whole, and complete already!

- **Action Step:** Hold your head up high, feeling sure that nothing is impossible for you. Act confident. Say the above affirmation at least 15 times a day.

HEALING PRACTICE #4

- **Sacred Scripture:** *Islam—Quran 48:4.* "He it is who sent down peace of reassurance into the hearts of believers, that they might add faith to their faith." Also, *Judaism—Isaiah 26:3.* "God keeps him in perfect peace whose mind is focused on Him."

- **Reflection:** *Peace* is one of those words I hunger to feel as an experienced reality in my life. For as long as I can remember, tension and stress have run my life. No wonder there has been a lot of disease in my body over the years. I must work on being more peaceful and believe that everything will turn out all right.

- **Prayer:** God, enable me to keep a steady focus on Your presence in my life so that Your peace will replace the tension and stress that have been with me for too long. Funny, even as I pray, I sense peace flowing throughout my body. Thank You, God.

- **Affirmation:** I rejoice, for I am filled with the peace of God as Divine Love controls my life.

- **Action Step:** Think of some past event in your life that creates anxiety for you even now. Think of the people involved and silently pray, "Peace be with you. I forgive you. I release you to be blessed with God's abundance."

HEALING PRACTICE #5

- **Sacred Scripture:** *Hinduism—Mundaka Upanishad 2.2.8.* "All evil effects of deeds are destroyed when he who is both person and impersonal is realized."

- **Reflection:** I think I have felt this personal Presence at times. There were times when I just knew that God was for *me*, and yet I also knew that God was all-inclusive. No matter what people believed or did, nobody was ever excluded from God's love. This is the truth I pray to have return to and fill me, because I know the power of such a truth to heal.

- **Prayer:** My heavenly Parent, restore to me the truth of Your personal and yet impersonal love, that I may live it always and practice it daily. Let me apply it to my own life as well as sharing it with others.

- **Affirmation:** I am greatly loved by God, and in return, I express that love to others.

- **Action Step:** Find a person in need of your love; undoubtedly, you know many people who could be in this category. Offer this person some expression of love. It might be personal or impersonal (such as an anonymous gift)—it certainly does not have to be some great, costly gesture. Just a simple expression will do.

HEALING PRACTICE #6

- **Sacred Scripture:** *Islam—Quran 11:114.* "Establish regular prayer at the two ends of the day and at the approaches of the night; for those things that are good remove those that are evil."

- **Reflection:** What a beautiful sentiment: To pray at the beginning and end of the day to repair the damage brought about by adverse energetics, such as negative and hateful thoughts. Sometimes these negative thoughts come before I even know it. I want to learn to control these kinds of thoughts before they burst forth into words and hurt others as well as myself. Is this possible?

- **Prayer:** Dear God, it is Your will that we love one another as we love ourselves. Help me to accept and love myself authentically and unconditionally. I do know that a great place to begin would be to stop negatively criticizing myself, judging myself so harshly, and to become more patient with who I am now. Let me accept what is.

- **Affirmation:** I am worthy of all God's blessings, including love, because I am lovable.

- **Action Step:** With an act of will, accept someone today who has been difficult for you to tolerate in the past. Remember, you are not accepting their negative behavior, but accepting them as one of God's children.

HEALING PRACTICE #7

- **Sacred Scripture:** *Buddhism, Sutta Pitaka.* "As a mother with her own life guards the life of her own child, let all-embracing thoughts for all that lives be thine."

- **Reflection:** There is no doubt that I ought to feel this way toward others, but sometimes it seems so unrealistic to me. Maybe I should ask myself, "*Why* does this seem unrealistic to me?" On a deeper level, I may need help to feel that I am included in the all-embracing thoughts of others . . . and God.

- **Prayer:** O God, Creator of all good, increase within me the sense of oneness with all Your creation. Help me be reverent toward all beings. Grant that I may use wisdom in utilizing the resources of nature. Help me show respect toward You by respecting Your creation—all of it!

- **Affirmation:** God is good, all creation is good, I am good, and all good deserves respect.

- **Action Step:** Begin by showing respect for the creation of God by carefully throwing away refuse in a respectful way. Today, if you see any improperly discarded trash, you can show prayerful respect for the planet by disposing of it properly.

HEALING PRACTICE #8

- **Sacred Scripture:** *Christianity—Luke 7:50.* "Jesus said to the women, 'Your faith has healed you. Enter into peace and experience freedom from all your distress.'"

- **Reflection:** Distress comes on many levels and in many forms: physical, emotional, mental, relational, and so on. Just thinking of this list is enough to distress me; even watching the evening news can upset me. What can I do?

- **Prayer:** God, You are the Lord of the present moment who soothes the distressed and gives them courage and strength. Your will is our health and wellness—help me to receive it now.

- **Affirmation:** I am free of distress because I am made in God's image, which is peace.
- **Action Step:** Do not watch the news on TV or

read the newspaper today. Instead, use this time to pray for the people who are in a state of misery. Through prayer, be a channel of peace for the suffering.

HEALING PRACTICE #9

- **Sacred Scripture:** *Christianity—Ephesians 4:23-24.* "Be constantly renewed in the spirit of your mind, having a fresh mental and spiritual attitude, and put on the new nature, which is created in God's image." Also, *Christianity—Romans 12:2.* "Be transformed by the renewing of your thinking and your attitudes."

- **Reflection:** In nature, we see the transformation of the caterpillar to the butterfly, but is this possible for humans? Can our nature be so changed that people find it difficult to recognize us? I know some people for whom this has happened. They do not seem to me to be the person they used to be. They are so much happier and more peaceful. And so, I would have to admit this kind of change *is* possible, even if I don't understand it.

- **Prayer:** Holy Spirit, you are the sacred transformer of our nature. You are our spiritual therapist who causes the change to take place where it really counts, in our inner being. I give you, Holy Spirit, full permission to help me rise above the caterpillar stage to become a butterfly. Come, Holy Spirit.

- **Affirmation:** The Holy Spirit is at work in me now, renewing me, reviving me, transforming me into the elegant spirit I was created to be.

- **Action Step:** Work on your attitude today by observing the attitudes of others. Decide which image you desire to portray: positive or negative, joyful or sad, strong or weak, complaining or uplifting. The choice is yours.

HEALING PRACTICE #10

- **Sacred Scripture:** *Judaism—Hosea 6:1–2.* "Come let us return to the Lord . . . that he may heal us . . . that we may live before him."

- **Reflection:** What a marvelous thought and desire that God might heal me. So often, fears concerning my lack of worthiness to be healed overwhelm me. How good do I have to be in order to be healed? Wouldn't it be great if my healing didn't depend on being a perfect human? Maybe it doesn't!

- **Prayer:** God, with all of my imperfections, I reach out to You, seeking healing. Somehow I do know that I don't have to be without blemish to get You to love and heal me. Help me to know this to be true.

- **Affirmation:** I walk in Divine Love this day, knowing that nothing can separate me from my God.

- **Action Step:** Sit comfortably for two or three minutes in this awareness. Then, express your gratitude that this is so. Whenever you doubt God's love for you, stop for a minute, take a deep breath, and silently affirm: *God loves me at all times*. Then go on about your day.

HEALING PRACTICE #11

- **Sacred Scripture:** *Buddhism—Sutta Nipata, 1146.* "By faith you shall be free and go beyond the world of death."

- **Reflection:** Faith! There's that word again. The word that brings such confusion and consternation to my mind. My belief system is so fragmented because of this word: In school, it meant one thing; in church, it meant another; at home, still another. Does it really have that much to do with religious dogma, or is faith about trust, confidence, even self-confidence? This is an area I really need to work on and determine whether or not "my" beliefs are truly my own.

- **Prayer:** I believe, Lord; help my unbelief. My greatest desire is to be confident of Your love for me so it will stimulate the healing energies I need to experience in my inner being.

- **Affirmation:** I am confident of this one thing, that God who began the good work in me is bringing it to completion now.

- **Action Step:** Invest some time over the next few days observing the doubtful thoughts that enter your mind, especially doubts about yourself and your God-given abilities. Notice without judgment whether these doubts cause you to be frustrated, angry, and fearful. Know for the time being that these feelings are normal and human, but at the same time, commit these feelings to the healing presence of God, your heavenly Father/Mother.

About Ron Roth, Ph.D.

Ron Roth, Ph.D., is an internationally known teacher, spiritual healer, and modern-day mystic. He has appeared on many TV and radio programs, including *The Oprah Winfrey Show*. Ron is the author of several books, including the best-seller *The Healing Path of Prayer*, and the audio-cassette *Healing Prayers*. He served in the Roman Catholic priesthood for more than 25 years and is the founder of Celebrating Life Institutes in Peru, Illinois, where he lives.

About Peter Occhiogrosso

Peter Occhiogrosso has been a journalist for more than 30 years and has written or co-written many books about world religion and spirituality, including his popular guide to the world's religious traditions, *The Joy of Sects*. He also coauthored *The Healing Path of Prayer, Prayer and the Five Stages of Healing,* and *Holy Spirit: The Boundless Energy of God* with Ron Roth. You can learn more about Peter at his Website, **joyofsects.com**.

∽ ∾

For more information on Ron Roth's Spiritual Healing Retreats, Holistic Spirituality Five-Day Intensives, Workshops, and Seminars, or to send in your Prayer Request and be placed on his mailing list, please visit Ron Roth's Website at **ronroth.com,** or use the address below:

Celebrating Life!
P.O. Box 428
Peru, IL 61354
e-mail: **ronroth@theramp.net**
Fax: 815-224-3395

For information on personal appointments with Ron Roth, or private phone sessions with Paul Funfsinn, please call (800) 814-4036.

∽ ∾

The Following Materials Are
Available Through Celebrating Life!:

BOOKS

The Healing Path of Prayer,
with Peter Occhiogrosso

AUDIOS

The Biology of Prayer, with Caroline Myss

Celebrate Life: Choices That Heal,
with Paul Funfsinn

*Divine Dialogue: How to Reclaim
Your Spiritual Power*

Forgiveness Therapy: A Christ-Centered Approach

Heal Your Life: Consciousness and Energy Medicine

Healing Meditation and Affirmations

Invoking the Sacred, with Caroline Myss

*The Lord's Prayer: Teachings
on the Our Father in Aramaic*

The Path to Answered Prayer

Prayer and Spirit As Energy Medicine

Reclaiming Your Spiritual Power

Spiritual Exploration: Navigating the Dark Night, with Caroline Myss

Taking Control of Your Life's Direction

Transformed by Love: The Healing Power of Authentic Self-Love

VIDEOCASSETTES

Praying with Power for Healing Guidance, Abundance, and Relationships

Spiritual Healing: Merging Mysticism and Meditation with Medicine

ADDITIONAL TOOLS FOR HEALING:
Designed by Ron Roth

Essential Oil: "Mystical Rose"
Ingredients: Pure Rose,
Sandalwood, Amber, and Musk

Mala Prayer Beads Bracelet: Eleven Quality
Gemstones with Instructions

Other Hay House Titles
of Related Interest

BOOKS

The Body "Knows": *How to Tune In to*
Your Body and Improve Your Health,
by Caroline Sutherland, Medical Intuitive

Eating in the Light: *Making the Switch to*
Vegetarianism on Your Spiritual Path,
by Doreen Virtue, Ph.D.,
and Becky Prelitz, M.F.T., R.D.

"Life Was Never Meant to Be a Struggle!"
by Stuart Wilde

Meditation: *Achieving Inner Peace*
and Tranquility in Your Life,
by Brain L. Weiss, M.D. (book and CD)

The Meditation Book, by John Randolph Price

Meditations, by Sylvia Browne

We hope you enjoyed this Hay House book.
If you would like to receive a free catalog featuring
additional Hay House books and products, or if
you would like information about the
Hay Foundation, please contact:

Hay House, Inc.
P.O. Box 5100
Carlsbad, CA 92018-5100

(760) 431-7695 or **(800) 654-5126**
(760) 431-6948 (fax) or **(800) 650-5115 (fax)**
www.hayhouse.com

Hay House Australia Pty Ltd
P.O. Box 515
Brighton-Le-Sands, NSW 2216
phone: 1800 023 516
e-mail: info@hayhouse.com.au